ROMANCE STUDIES

Romance Studies

Presented to

William Morton Dey
Kenan Professor of Romance Languages

on the Occasion of his Seventieth Birthday

by His Colleagues and Former Students

Edited by Urban T. Holmes, Jr., Alfred G. Engstrom
and Sturgis E. Leavitt

CHAPEL HILL
1950

Copyright 1950
By the University of North Carolina
Chapel Hill, N. C.

Table of Contents

Vita and Bibliography
9

A Note on Larra's *No más mostrador*
Nicholson B. Adams
15

Rationalization and Realization in the Characters of Racine
Raymond Andes
21

A Comment on Luzán's Observations on the Spanish *Comedia*
J. Worth Banner
29

Two Notes on Enrique Amorim, Uruguayan *Cuentista* and Novelist
L. L. Barrett
35

Mark the Boat
R. S. Boggs
43

A Possible Source for Hugo's "Three Ages of Poetry"
John A. Downs
51

Lucretius and *Micromégas*
Alfred G. Engstrom
59

A Note on Old French *bliaut*
Rosalyn Gardner
63

Romance Languages in North Carolina, 1909-1949
Hugo Giduz
69

A Note on the Word *Fauve* in Old French
Marion A. Greene
75

Charles Péguy et la mystique française
Jacques Hardré
81

A Troubadour Lesson in Practical Semantics
Elliott Dow Healy
89

The Dominican Rite and the Judaeo-Christian Theory of the Grail
Urban T. Holmes, Jr.
95

Jean-Jacques Rousseau and Anatole France
Howard R. Huse
101

Elements of White Magic in Mediaeval Spanish *Exempla*
John E. Keller
107

Did Calderón Have a Sense of Humor?
Sturgis E. Leavitt
119

A Comic Enchantment in the *Perceforest*
Robert G. Lewis
125

Non-Classical French Criticism in the Mid-Seventeenth Century:
Charles Sorel and his *Bibliothèque françoise*
J. C. Lyons
131

Louisiana-French Loan Words for 'Water-Fowl'
in the Spanish of St. Bernard Parish, Louisiana
Raymond R. MacCurdy
139

The Use of *Vos* in Panamanian Spanish
Stanley L. Robe
145

Preconception of Reality, and Abulia, in Nineteenth-century
French Decadent Literature
James M. Smith
153

A Note on Scott in Spain
Sterling A. Stoudemire
165

The Critics and *O Missionario*
Don H. Walther
171

A Note on the Identity of Marie de France
Rogers Dey Whichard
177

A Defense of the Renaissance *Gentilhomme Champêtre*
W. L. Wiley
185

Sarrazins Espans in the *Roland*, vv. 269, 612, 2828
William S. Woods
193

Vita and Bibliography

VITA AND BIBLIOGRAPHY

William Morton Dey, the son of George W. Dey, was born in Norfolk, Va., on June 23rd, 1880. His family was an outstanding one in the community, imbued with those Virginia traditions which have bred cosmopolitan leadership in the South. After his graduation from the Norfolk Academy, in 1897, William Dey spent a year at the University of North Carolina, in Chapel Hill, where his mother's brother, Walter Dallam Toy, was head of the Department of Modern Languages. In 1898 young Dey transferred to the University of Virginia and received his A.B. and an A. M. from that Institution, both in the year 1902. He entered Harvard University in 1903, and there, in 1904, he was given a second A. M. degree; in 1906 he was awarded the Ph.D. During his final year at Harvard University he was an Austin Teaching Fellow.

Professor Dey's first post after leaving the Graduate School was at the University of Missouri where he was an Assistant Professor of French, associated with Raymond Weeks. When Professor Weeks left the department in 1908 it was W. M. Dey who succeeded as executive officer. The lure of the Atlantic seaboard is always strong for a native of Virginia. In 1909 it was decided at Chapel Hill to split the old Department of Modern Languages into a Department of German and a Department of Romance Languages. Walter Dallam Toy continued to head the Department of German and Mr. Dey was invited to be the first head of the Department of Romance Languages. There were only two other members of the Department and the three men cared for Spanish and Italian, as well as for French. Conditions were soon ideal for rapid growth. Under the leadership of Edwin Greenlaw and of Francis P. Venable the Graduate School in Arts and Sciences continued to increase and the Department of Romance Languages contributed fully to this expansion. The Philological Club, which had come into existence in 1893, founded a journal in 1906 which was called *Studies in Philology*. Mr. Dey played a major role in getting this project under way. On December 28, 1910, Professor Dey married Ellen Alice Old of Norfolk, Va. In 1918 he began to live in the house on the northeast corner of Rosemary Lane and Hillsboro St., a fine old residence which will long be remembered as the Dey house.

The First World War contributed still further to the expansion of the University of North Carolina. William Dey had begun his career as an Old French scholar, but his interest had gradually centered on the Romantic Movement in France with special emphasis on Alfred de Vigny. A second scholarly interest was Phonetics, which attracted his attention considerably after 1912. In 1920-1921 Professor Dey spent the year in France at the University of Paris. The Department of Romance Languages at Chapel Hill had awarded an A. M. degree in 1912, but a swift advance in graduate instruction was noted in 1924 when five A.M. degrees were given at a single Commencement. The first Ph.D. degree was granted to John Coriden Lyons in 1928. The Department developed rapidly after that date and was soon on its way to being one of the major departments of Romance Languages in the country. In 1934 Professor Dey was promoted to a Kenan professorship of the Romance Languages and Literatures. From 1935-1940 he was Chairman of the Division of Humanities. During the Second World War most of the staff were away in government service. Professor Dey held the fort in Murphey 213 and 214, in a building which was given over almost entirely to the Navy. The staff began to trickle back early in 1945, and it was not long before the Department was even more active than it had been before the War.

On December 10th, 1949, William Morton Dey received a greatly coveted honor. He was awarded the cross of Chevalier of the Legion of Honor by Consul-General Jean Strauss of the French Republic. The occasion was a memorable one, and the large number of faculty members and other friends present was an eloquent symbol of affectionate esteem for a man whose grace, personality, and integrity of character have meant so much to his Department and his University.

Professor Dey is a member of the Modern Language Association of America, the South Atlantic Modern Language Association, the American Association of Teachers of French, and Phi Beta Kappa. He belongs also to a Junior Order at the University of North Carolina which is called Gorgon's Head, and to the Delta Kappa Epsilon Fraternity.

BIBLIOGRAPHY

"French and Spanish Pronunciation," *North Carolina High School Bulletin*, I (1910), 138-40.

"The Teaching of Pronunciation of the Modern Languages," *North Carolina High School Bulletin*, IV (1913), 164.

"The Latin Prefix *Pro-* in French," *Studies in Philology*, XII (1915), 138-82.

Editor of *Adolphe*, by Benjamin Constant. New York: Oxford University Press, 1918. Pp. xxii, 164.

"A Note on Old French *Por-* in English," *Studies in Philology*, XVII (1920), 111-12.

(With André Béziat) *French Grammar*. Richmond (Virginia): Johnson Publishing Company, 1927. Pp. 537.

"A Note on Stendhal and Victor Hugo," *Studies in Philology*, XXVIII (1931), 306-08.

"The Pessimism and Optimism of Alfred de Vigny," *Studies in Philology*, XXXIII (1936), 405-16.

"The Beginnings of the Philological Club," *The University of North Carolina Record*, No. 283 (1942), 7-13.

"The History of *Studies in Philology*," *Studies in Philology*, XLII (1945), 381-84.

"Alfred de Vigny, Romantic Poet," in *Lectures in the Humanities: Second Series. 1945-1946* (University of North Carolina Extension Bulletin, XXVI [1946], 3-15.)

A Note on Larra's *No mas mostrador*

A NOTE ON LARRA'S NO MAS MOSTRADOR
Nicholson B. Adams

Students and biographers of Larra have all had something to say about his first play,[1] but one or two facts in connection with it have remained unnoticed. We know that Larra was introduced to the stage by Juan Grimaldi, and his play, first performed at the Teatro de la Cruz on April 29, 1831, was entitled *No más mostrador*. It was presented anonymously, but Larra, after witnessing its favorable reception, acknowledged his authorship in a letter to the editor of the *Correo Literario y Mercantil* for May 4.[2] The play was published in 1831, and again in 1836 and in 1843 and in various collections of Larra's works, always with the description "Comedia original en cinco actos," with Larra's name.

All agree that the play was popular. It may be interesting to see just how popular. It was shown in Madrid in 1831, always at the Cruz, on April 29, 30, May 1, 5, 6, 8, 9, 10, 27, June 27, December 12, 13, 18. For the times, that is a very respectable number of performances indeed. It was definitely one of the most popular plays of the year. It was shown six times in 1833, and twice in 1834. It was also presented in Seville and Cadiz.[3]

Most of the discussion of the play has revolved around the question of its originality, and with good reason. Bretón de los Herreros, in his excellent review[4] in the *Correo*, was the first to comment on this "original" comedy at an epoch when the Spanish stage was flooded with translations and operas: "Si en todos los tiempos ha sido grata a los amantes de nuestra literatura dramática la aparición en escena de una obra original, necesariamente ha de serlo mucho más en nuestros días." On May 10, in *Cartas Españolas,* Jose María Carnerero (now on good terms with Larra, who had before vigorously attacked him in *El Duende Satírico del Día*) in reviewing the play,[5] speaks of its "rasgos de mucha originalidad," and closes his review thus: "En una época en que la literatura dramática está tan decaída, escribir esta comedia, es empezar por donde otros quisieran concluir. C[arnerero]."

Larra accepted these tributes. No one publicly questioned the originality of the play for about three years. In the *Diario de Comercio* for March 22, 1834, an anonymous author who calls himself "El Amigo de la Verdad" stated in effect that *No más mostrador* was a translation of Scribe and Mélesville's *Comédie-vaudeville* called *Les adieux au comptoir*. Larra replied the very next day in the *Revista Española* with a long and proud *Vindicación*.[6]

The plays in question, by Scribe-Mélesville and by Larra, are readily accessible to those who wish to compare them, and they have already been discussed. Suffice it to say, then, in brief, that in *Les adieux au comptoir* we have a dry goods merchant and his wife who have grown rich in trade. The wife, however, wishes to retire, to move to a better street (the Chaussée d'Antin) and to marry their daughter to a nobleman. The merchant wishes to marry her to a young merchant. Mother and daughter happen to have met a charming young man who remained anonymous, at a dance, and they were delighted with his good looks and his elegance. The merchant's son reveals to the father that he was the young man, and that he is most anxious to marry the girl. The father persuades him to masquerade as a count. The father happens to know that the real count will be out of Paris for a few hours, and he even hires the count's "jockey" (groom) to help the plot. At the proper juncture the young man reveals his identity, the real count is discovered to be a worthless spend-thrift, the daughter is happy, and the mother yields, though not with good grace. The last line of the father's triumphant song is: "Ne faites pas vos adieux au comptoir."

Larra, hispanising the characters and the locale (Madrid) uses precisely the same situations and parallels the dialogue through his second act. Then he adds a touch: he brings on the real count, and the audience sees the count masquerading as the young merchant, and the young merchant masquerading as the count, at the same time and in the same house. In short, an intrigue like some of the more exaggerated *Siglo de Oro* comedies, such as *Don Gil de las calzas verdes*. Larra's count is a worthless and cowardly scoundrel, and the girl marries the young merchant with joy. The mother is cured of her follies, and all look forward to a happy life in an honorable trade. Other similarities and other differences of detail could be pointed out.

Miss MacGuire[7] and Carmen de Burgos[8] agree that, along broad lines, Larra had a right to call his play original. Mr. Hespelt[9] very charitably says: "if we allow, then, a very broad use of the adjective, we may consider Larra justified in calling *No más mostrador* original."

Larra's own *Vindicación*, however, displays more haughtiness than passion for strict truthfulness. The most significant section is this:

> Deseando probar mis fuerzas en el arte dramático hace algunos años, y a la sazón que buscaba asunto para una comedia, cayó en mis manos aquel *vaudeville* en un *acto corto* de Scribe. Presumiendo por mis limitados conocimientos que no podría ser de ningún efecto en los teatros de Madrid apoderéme de la idea, y haciéndola mía por derecho de conquista, escribí el *No más mostrador, en cinco actos largos*; hice más: habiendo encontrado en Scribe dos o tres escenas que desconfié de escribir mejor, las aproveché, llevado también de la poca importancia que en mi cuadro iban a tener. Yo no sé si esto se puede hacer, lo que sé es que yo lo he hecho. Dióse la comedia en cinco actos, traducida literalmente, según el amigo de la verdad, de la *comedia en un acto*, y tuvo la buena suerte de agradar.

Larra's statement that he made Scribe's idea his own "by right of conquest" is airily put, surely. And instead of two or three scenes, as he says, he closely paralleled twelve. It is true that Larra's play is much longer, but it is not true that Scribe's one act is short, or that each of Larra's five is long. Scribe's one act is approximately as long as any two of Larra's. The Spanish author may or may not have been right in one statement about his comedy: "... buena o mala, no creo que su éxito se haya debido a lo que hay de Scribe en ella." The defects of characterization and motivation pointed out by Bretón and Carnerero, however, apply to Larra's part, not to Scribe's.

In 1831 and 1832 the theatrical notices announced *No más mostrador* simply as a *comedia en cinco actos*, with no author's name. In fact, it was extremely rare that the name of any author should be mentioned. However, for the performance in 1834, after Larra's brush with his anonymous attacker, the announcement read thus: *No Más Mostrador de Mariano José de Larra (Fígaro)*. One strongly suspects that Larra insisted on the notice in that form.

Larra's general attitude toward Scribe is worth noting. In his article *La vida de Madrid*[10] he comments with at least a slight tone of protest on the tremendous popularity of Scribe on the Madrid stage:

> — ¿ Que se da en el teatro? dice uno...
> — Aquí: 1° sinfonía; 2° pieza del célebre Scribe: 3° sinfonía; 4° pieza nueva del fecundo Scribe; 5° sinfonía; 6° baile nacional; 7° la comedia nueva en dos actos, traducida también del ingenioso Scribe; 8° sinfonía; 9° ...
> — Basta, basta; ¡Santo Dios!

In the article *Una primera representación*,[11] Larra, listing the sorts of dramatic fare on the Madrid stage, says:

> ... hay la piececita de costumbres, sin costumbres, traducción de Scribe: insulsa a veces, graciosita a ratos, ingeniosa por aquí y por allí ...

Well, Larra was one of many who turned an honest *real* translating or adapting plays of Scribe, and thereby increasing the Frenchman's vogue in Spain. No matter what he said or thought about Scribe, Larra translated or adapted no less than ten of his plays! They are: *No más mostrador, Felipe, Julia, Siempre, Las desdichas de un amante dichoso, El arte de conspirar, Partir a tiempo, Tu amor o la muerte, La madrina, Los inseparables.*

We may add a note here to show a disservice to "Fígaro" by his great admirer Carmen de Burgos. She says: "Antes de su viaje al extranjero había estrenado 'Fígaro' en 1832, el 28 de febrero, con el seudónimo de Ramón de Arriala, en el teatro del Príncipe, una traducción del francés, que se ha dado como original, intitulado *Felipe* . . ." For one thing, it was first presented Feb. 25 (and Feb. 26 and March 1). *Otelo, tragedia en 5 actos* was played at the Príncipe on Feb. 28. Furthermore, *Felipe* is not announced in the Gaceta as a *comedia original,* but *simply* as *a comedia en 2 actos.* Moreover, the catalogue of the *Biblioteca Municipal de Madrid* lists the play thus: "Felipe. Co. 2 actos, pros., por M. Scribe. Arreglada al teatro esp. por D. Ramón Arriala 1832. Ms. 4."

Apparently this time, as in subsequent cases, Larra admits his indebtedness. His translations were unimportant in comparison with his extraordinarily keen critical articles, and he did not need to claim any credit which was not completely due him.

The University of North Carolina

---

[1] The more significant studies are: Carmen de Burgos (Colombine), *Fígaro"* (Madrid, 1919), pp. 78-79; Elizabeth MacGuire, *A Study of the Writings of D. Mariano José de Larra* (*University of California Publications,* VII, Berkeley, 1918), pp. 87-130; F. C. Tarr, "Larra: Nuevos datos críticos y literarios (1829-1833)," *Revue Hispanique,* LXXVII (1929), 246-69; E. Herman Hespelt, "The Translated Dramas of Mariano José de Larra and Their French Originals," *Hispania,* XV (1932), 117-34.
[2] See Tarr, *op cit.*, p. 255.
[3] Carmen de Burgos, *op. cit.*, p. 79.
[4] Quoted almost entire by Tarr, *op. cit.*, pp. 253-55.
[5] *Cartas Españolas,* I (1831), 118-19; also quoted by Tarr, *op cit.*, pp. 256-58.
[6] Reproduced by Carmen de Burgos, *op cit.*, pp. 78-79, and by E. Cotarelo, *Post-fígaro* (Madrid, 1918), II, 218-23.
[7] *Op. cit.*
[8] *Op. cit.*
[9] *Op. cit.*, pp. 120-21.
[10] First published in *El Observador* on Dec. 12, 1834.
[11] First published in *La Revista Española,* April 3, 1835.
[12] *Op. cit.*, p. 80.

Rationalization and Realization
In the Characters of Racine

RATIONALIZATION AND REALIZATION IN THE CHARACTERS OF RACINE

Raymond N. Andes

Racine made use of rationalization[1] so frequently in his tragedies that we conclude that the device intrigued him as well as modern psychologists. In his characters as well as in life, rationalization is a complex, "liquid" process in which the true reasons for the attitude or act often lie so near the surface of the conscious that they constantly emerge to dissipate the ones presented by the rationalizer. From this subtle process of rationalization and realization, the ebb and flow of the rational self, Racine lays bare the mental life and habits of his characters. For our purpose here we assume that when the irrelevant (but not necessarily false) reasons presented for any given act or attitude are viewed frankly in their true perspective, rationalization has ceased and realization has occurred.

Rationalization is essential to Racine's dramatic system. It is only human for individuals, when driven by powers or beset by circumstances over which they have little control, to use an escape mechanism to evade reality. Racine's impassioned characters find in rationalization a momentary and insecure mental haven, soon dissolved by themselves or others. Examples of this device are found in a number of Racine's plays, and several are of identical pattern.

In *Alexandre*, Act I, Scene 1, Taxile rationalizes, when, enamoured of the beautiful Axiane, he wishes to wage war against her enemy, Alexandre, for what appear to him true and altruistic reasons. Evidence that her affections point elsewhere is clear to all those who look upon the situation objectively, and Taxile's sister seeks to disclose the truth to him when she questions in utter amazement his doubt that Axiane has become the lover of Porus. That there is a small, and often nebulous, marginal area which distinguishes rationalization from realization is subtly implied in the reply of Taxile to his sister:

> Je tâchais d'en douter, cruelle Cléofile:
> Hélas! dans son erreur affermissez Taxile.
> Pourquoi lui peignez-vous cet objet odieux?
> Aidez-le bien plutôt à démentir ses yeux:
> Dites-lui qu'Axiane est une beauté fière,
> Telle à tous les mortels qu'elle est à votre frère;
> Flattez de quelque espoir . . .[2]

When Taxile suggests that he is in love with Axiane and that she is advocating armed resistance to Alexandre, we know that he is deceiving only himself as to his real motives. Yet they are so near the surface of the conscious that when his sister mercilessly analyzes the situation for him, recognition of his self-deception is forced upon him, and he names her "cruelle" for destroying his *protection against anxiety*.

Our dramatist presents us with an analogous situation in one of the finest scenes he wrote. Act II, Scene 1 of *Andromaque* is pregnant with psychological realism as Racine pitilessly dissects the soul of Hermione. Her true reason for remaining at the palace of Pyrrhus after he has repeatedly insulted her is that she cannot force herself to renounce all hope that Pyrrhus' love for her will return. This motivation, while in the subconscious, lies so near the conscious that the alternate advent and recession of her objective self can be traced with great delicacy. Racine reveals every nuance of Hermione's passion as she submits to herself and discards one reason after another explaining her continued presence. She finally undeceives herself concerning Pyrrhus only to take refuge in a new position as untenable as the previous ones.

Step by step, Racine leads us through her mental detours. When Cléone, her confidante, pleads with her to leave with Oreste, who really loves her, she improvises the first explanation:

> Ah! laisse à ma fureur le temps de croître encore;
> Contre mon ennemi laisse-moi m'assurer:
> Cléone, avec horreur je m'en veux séparer.
> Il n'y travaillera que trop bien, l'infidèle!

As Cléone remonstrates with her, Hermione confesses her self-deception, of which she has really been cognizant all along:

> Pourquoi veux-tu, cruelle, irriter mes ennuis?
> Je crains de me connoître en l'état où je suis.
> De tout ce que tu vois tâche de ne rien croire;
> Crois que je n'aime plus, vante-moi ma victoire;
> Crois que dans son dépit mon coeur est endurci;
> Hélas! et s'il se peut, fais-le-moi croire aussi.
> Tu veux que je le fuie. Hé bien! rien ne m'arrête:
> Allons.

But her mind, tortured by the thought of departure, cannot withstand, and so she invents another, less plausible reason for remaining:

> Fuyons... Mais si l'ingrat rentroit dans son devoir!
> Si la foi dans son coeur retrouvoit quelque place!

> S'il venoit à mes pieds me demander sa grâce!
> Si sous mes lois, Amour, tu pouvois l'engager!
> S'il vouloit . . .

The suppositions are more and more incredible, and the absurdity of the last one forces her to face reality again:

> . . . Mais l'ingrat ne veut que m'outrager.

However, a course of action consistent with reason is too unpleasant to contemplate:

> Demeurons toutefois pour troubler leur fortune;
> Prenons quelque plaisir à leur être importune;

Cléone shows her the injustice and uselessness of this idea, whereupon she accepts the bitter truth in regard to Pyrrhus but consoles herself with the thought that she may learn to love Oreste:

> Hermione est sensible, Oreste a des vertus.
> Il sait aimer du moins, et même sans qu'on l'aime;
> Et peut-être il saura se faire aimer lui-même.
> Allons: qu'il vienne enfin.

At his appearance she shows the artificiality of this escape mechanism with the simple but eloquent remark:

> Ah! je ne croyois pas qu'il fût si près d'ici .

A less complex case of rationalization and realization is found in the third act of *Phèdre* where Phèdre rationalizes the frigid reception given by Hippolyte to her confession of love for him:

> Oenone, il peut quitter cet orgueil qui te blesse.
> Nourri dans les forêts, il en a la rudesse.
> Hippolyte, endurci par de sauvages lois,
> Entend parler d'amour pour la première fois.
> Peut-être sa surprise a causé son silence; (ll. 781-86)

Realization comes to Phèdre after prodding by Oenone:

> Enfin tous tes conseils ne sont plus de saison.
> Sers ma fureur, Oenone, et non ma raison. (ll. 91-92)

It is significant that Racine relies upon rationalization and realization most often in *Bérénice*. Here where "toute l'invention consiste à faire quelque chose de rien" ("Préface"), where the extreme simplicity of plot and detail is matched only by an equal degree of psychological violence, Racine needed all his ingenuity to sustain interest.

Bérénice, having been informed by Antiochus that Titus has

decided to abandon his plan of marrying her, at first rejects, then concedes the truth of the information:

> Après tant de serments, Titus m'abandonner!
> Titus qui me juroit . . . Non, je ne le puis croire:
> Il ne me quitte point, il y va de sa gloire.
> Contre son innocence on veut me prévenir.
> Ce piège n'est tendu que pour nous désunir.
> Titus m'aime. Titus ne veut point que je meure. (ll. 906-11)

> Non, je ne vous crois point. Mais, quoi qu'il en puisse être,
> Pour jamais à mes yeux gardez-vous de paraître. (ll. 915-16)

> (A Phénice)
> Ne m'abandonne pas dans l'état où je suis.
> Hélas! pour me tromper je fais ce que je puis. (ll. 917-18)

Antiochus, forbidden to appear in her presence again, momentarily attempts to conceal the truth from himself as he echoes the words of Bérénice:

> Ne me trompé-je point? L'ai-je bien entendue?
> Que je me garde, moi, de paroître à sa vue! (ll. 919-20)

The nature and importance of rationalization-realization in Racine's tragedies are indicated by the representative examples quoted above.[3] The mechanism involved is not solely that of rationalization-realization, but even in the very complexity of the mental activity depicted, Racine proves his understanding of the phenomenon so fully studied and described by modern psychologists. He achieves unquestioned effectiveness by these explorations of the marginal state between the conscious and the subconscious. Thus, by the dramatic representation of subtle mental processes and violent conflicts within the individual as well as verbal dissentions among characters, he compensates for the absence of spectacle in his theatre. The successful depiction of any intellectual activity in which the mind moves from the vantage points of the subjective to the objective, the subconscious to the conscious, involves a percipient comprehension of the inner man. Racine was eminently skillful in portraying in his characters this psychological alchemy of the change from rationalization to realization.

Bridgewater College
Bridgewater, Virginia

---

[1] The word *rationalization* is employed in the technical psychological sense of ". . . the mental process of devising ostensible reasons, or motives to justify an act or opinion which is actually based on other motives or grounds . . ." (Ho-

ward C. Warren, *Dictionary of Psychology*, New York: Houghton Mifflin Co., 1934, p. 223). Psychologists agree that the underlying motivation *may be* unconscious and unknown to the individual [and one might then assume, conversely, that it *may be known* as well]. Rationalization is also described as a "protection against anxiety . . ." since it ". . . keeps the person from knowing those of his motives and wishes which are at variance with his ideal . . . concerning himself" (Lawrence I. O'Kelly, *Introduction to Psychopathology*, New York: Prentice-Hall, Inc., 1949, p. 495).

[2] Racine, *Théâtre complet de Racine* (Paris: Librairie Garnier Frères, s.d.). Hereafter all passages will be quoted from *Théâtre choisi de Racine* (Paris: Librairie Hachette, s.d.).

[3] Other instances of rationalization accompanied by varying degrees of realization are found in *Bérénice*, ll. 788-98, 1005-13; in *Andromaque*, ll. 33-86; in *Mithridate*, ll. 1000-10, 1147-80.

A Comment on Luzan's Observations
On the Spanish *Comedia*

A COMMENT ON LUZAN'S OBSERVATION ON THE SPANISH *COMEDIA*

J. Worth Banner

The increasing severity of Luzán's attack on the *comedia* of the Golden Age in the 1789 edition of his *Poética* over that contained in the first edition (1737) has received frequent comment. Luzán scores with considerable acerbity the unrestrained exuberance and non-classic characteristics of the *comedia* of this period. He calls to account both authors and plays in some detail, and lists among others the following as illustrating some of the most common defects characteristic of the *comedia* of the period:

Calderón de la Barca. *Fortunas de Andrómeda y Perseo, Mujer llora, vencerás, Para vencer amor querer vencerle, Dicha y desdicha del nombre, En esta vida todo es verdad y todo mentira, Armas de la hermosura, Duelos de amor y lealtad, Conde Lucanor, Gran Zenobia,* and *La gran reina de Saba.*

Lope de Vega. *El amigo hasta la muerte, El perro del hortelano, Los ramilletes de Madrid, La locura por la honra, El mayordomo de la duquesa de Amalfi,* and *El príncipe perfecto.*

Antonio Moreto, Antonio Solís, and Juan de Matos Fragoso are among others who serve as targets for the critical darts of Luzán. In the case of the last named author he even goes so far as to speak with a notable lack of classic *mesure* and with considerable vigor: ". . . Juan de Matos Fragoso de cuya pluma jamás se deslizó una expresión natural . . ."[1]

However, despite the increasing severity of Luzán's criticism of the *comedia* in this second edition of the *Poética*, he was not blinded to its positive values, as were so many of his neo-Classic compatriots in the eighteenth century. Even though in his censure he names more of Calderón's plays than those of any other author, at the same time he pays considerable tribute to this great figure of the Golden Age of Spanish literature.

> . . . . por lo que mira al arte, no se puede negar que sin sujetarse Calderón a las justas reglas de los antiguos, hay en algunas de sus comedias el arte primero de todos, que es el de interesar a los espectadores o lectores . . . . circumstancia esencialísima de que no se pueden gloriar muchos poetas de otras naciones grandes observadores de las reglas.[2]

Luzán's recognition of the ability of the author to interest the spectators or readers as primary artistry is particularly interesting, since the general lack of this ability is so glaringly evident among the Spanish neo-Classic dramatists.

Luzán continues in a laudatory vein: "... conserva Calderón casi todo su primitivo aplauso: sirvió y sirve de modelo; y son sus comedias el caudal más redituable de nuestros."[3] This comment serves as additional testimony of the failure of Spanish neo-Classicism in the field of the drama.

It is interesting to note at this point that Luzán makes no mention whatsoever of either Tirso de Molina or Juan Ruiz de Alarcón. It seems strange indeed that in treating the drama of the Golden Age he would leave unmentioned two of the four greatest dramatists of the period. Particularly is this so in the case of Alarcón. It would seem that the latter's care in workmanship and certain inclination toward some of the regulatory precepts of neo-Classicism would have occasioned laudatory comment on the part of Luzán. However, such was not the case.

One form of the *comedia*, though, does bring forth unstinted praise from the Spanish neo-Classicist: the *comedia de figurón*. It is for this form of the *comedia* that Luzán expresses his most unqualified admiration:

> ... se hicieron desde entonces más frecuentes las que propiamente son comedias: esto es las que llaman de figurón porque pintan y ridiculizan los vicios o sandeces de alguna persona extravagante. No diré que en estas comedias falte que corregir ni que contienen todas las circunstancias constitutivas de la perfección; pero van camino de ella, y tienen mucho de lo que llamaban los antiguos *vis comica*.[4]

Examples of this dramatic form which he deems worthy of note are mentioned as follows: Francisco de Rojas Zorrilla's *Don Lucas del Cigarral*, Juan de la Hoz's *El castigo de la miseria*, Antonio de Solís's *Un bobo hace ciento*, Antonio de Zamora's *Hechizado por fuerza*, and José de Cañizares's *El dómine Lucas*.

As a result of all the emphasis which has been laid on the severity of Luzán's censure of the *comedia* of the Golden Age in the second edition of the *Poética*, it should not be overlooked that his criticism was not a blanket condemnation of a literary genre. He found much therein to be admired and much of positive literary value. It is a tribute to his critical acumen that in the midst of the heated controversy between the neo-Classicists and traditionalists he was able to maintain to a certain degree a dispassionate objectivity in his literary judgments. Luzan's aesthetic and literary senses were too mature to permit him to descend to pure emotionalism as a sole basis of literary judgment.

In reading Luzan's criticism, one is ever conscious of the ideal combination of sound common sense and a profound cultural background. Whether we agree with them or not, his judgments reflect reasoned criteria. He makes no breastbeating defense of a literary cause; and even when his opinions are severely critical, they are quite obviously born of a contemplative reflection based on a sound cultural foundation. The field of literary criticism was well served in the contributions of this very learned and distinguished gentleman.

College of William and Mary

[1] Ignacio de Luzán, *La poética, o reglas de la poesía en general y de sus principales especies* (Madrid, 1789), II, 33.
[2] *Op cit.*, p. 30.
[3] *Loc. cit.*
[4] *Op. cit.*, pp. 35-36.

Two Notes on Enrique Amorim, Uruguayan *Cuentista* and Novelist

TWO NOTES ON ENRIQUE AMORIM URUGUAYAN *CUENTISTA* AND NOVELIST

L. L. Barrett

I. "Quitanderas"

Amorim's first volume of fiction introduces, in the fourteenth of its short stories, a social type of such originality that it has aroused much discussion in Uruguay and Argentina, caused two repercussions in France, and coincides oddly with a recently published fact in the United States. "Las quitanderas" as used by Amorim is a term unknown prior to the appearance of his book in 1923.[1] Lexicographers and sociologists agree that no such women as those Amorim portrays have ever been seen on the Uruguayan pampa, and that therefore the word applied to these female personages is entirely new. Evidently, then, Amorim has created, not merely interpreted. As the creator of both type and term he defines the latter at the head of the story: "Quitandera: En América, a la vagabunda amorosa de los callejones patrios." A more delicately phrased and specific definition occurs in the Parisian magazine *Candide*: ". . . un personnage féminin inventé de toutes pièces: pour adoucir la solitude des gauchos dans la Pampa, des femmes, les Quitanderas, s'en allaient, amoureuse caravane, offrir une passagère tendresse aux grands solitaires de la plaine argentine" [*sic*].[2]

That Amorim has thereafter been proudly conscious of the originality of his creation is clearly seen in certain of his later productions. One of the figures in *Tangarupá*,[3] a short novel, is the *curandera* Misia Felipa, who "vivía rodeada de hijastros y guachitos. Recogía los hijos abandonados, para criarlos a su modo, y más de una quitandera había encomendado a sus manos el fruto de sus pobres amores de vagabundas." The word *quitandera* is neither italicized nor enclosed in quotation marks; its status is evidently regarded by the author as naturalizado si no native (the most probable source is the Brazilian *quitandeira*). In the first short story of the same book, "Quitanderas (segundo episodio)," Amorim returns to the subject, and seven years later brings out the novel *La carreta*, the full-length history of the ambulant brothel and its women.[4] Commenting on the success of this novel five years afterwards, the novelist confirms his pride in his creation: "A mí solo me cabe la certeza de que las 'quitanderas' han existido en mi imaginación, por el hecho cabal de haberles dado vida en páginas novelescas."[5]

There is justification for the boast. Amorim reprints scholarly articles from his own region as proof, and adds items from Parisian journals to show that the arts have paid him the tribute of imitation: a French writer turns out a novel in which Amorim's personages are used and which even bears the title *La quitandera* (the Uruguayan calls it, mildly enough, "plagio inocente"); and a painter exhibits a whole series of pictures of *quitanderas* in Paris.[6] There, at least, Amorim's fictional invention has taken on the semblance of fact; for some individuals the *quitanderas* are creatures of flesh and blood as well as of paper and ink.

The action of *La carreta* takes place in a period intentionally made indeterminate. Its *terminus ad quem* may be set as the date when automobiles first appeared on Uruguay's back roads, but its *terminus a quo* is far less definite. The *carreta* may conceivably have creaked on its way at any time since such two-wheeled, covered wagons were first used, so that its date of existence (fictional) may even have coincided with the existence (real) of analogous women in our country.

That such women did indeed ply their trade in like fashion on our midwestern plains is attested by William Allen White, who says that when he was six or seven years old (or around 1874-1875),

> . . . one summer day we discovered a camping place deep in the woods above the town [Eldorado, Kansas] where there was often a covered wagon and some strange girls. We used to peek through the brush at what was going on there until Merz Young, who was the protector of the innocent, came and chased us off with yells and curses, throwing rocks. And the knowledge of good and evil came to us, even as to the Pair in the Garden.[7]

The similarity of the fictional social type invented by Amorim for the pampa of Uruguay to the real one on the Kansas plains, even to the detail of the covered wagon, is remarkable.

II. Self-plagiarism?

La carreta is an episodic novel, its fragmentary elements linked into a continuous chain more by the wagon itself than by the personnel of its passengers, for one of these may drop out and be replaced from time to time. Some part of the cause for the episodic nature of the story may be Amorim's procedure in fashioning the whole from a few pieces. For the novel he not only uses the first *quitandera* story published, inserting it as Chapter IX, but also appropriates the "segundo episodio" from the volume *Tangarupá* to begin at Chapter XIV and continue to the end of the book. Since these tales directly involve *quitanderas*, they fit neatly into the scheme of the novel, which indeed may have been constructed with them as the nucleus around which all the rest is organized. But not even all the rest is new material. Having removed one story from *Tangarupá*, Amorim simply lifts the two remaining from that book, introducing "El pájaro negro" as Chapter XI and "Los explotadores de pantanos" as Chapter XIII. Both stories being accounts of types peculiar to the region, and thus potentially in contact with *quitanderas*, they lend themselves well to their new use.

Still, these earlier pieces rarely appear in their new settings without alterations, in either diction or detail of fact, necessitated by the exigencies of the longer framework. For example, the Ford of the original story becomes a buggy (*volanta*) in Chapter XIII of the novel, a change that eliminates the need for the doctor's chauffeur. It is the buggy's owner who drives the physician in that vehicle to attend the sick wife. And so on. The changes mentioned suggest the probable source of a sequence in the action of another novel, *El caballo y su sombra*,[8] the tragically frustrated effort of Toribio Rossi to carry his diphtheria-stricken child to a doctor. It is the basic idea, rather than any particular details, that coincides in the two passages to suggest that once again Amorim has had recourse to his own work. The same novel turns upon the pivotal device of an expensive horse whose metaphorical shadow touches the action and characters to precipitate the climax. A like device in an earlier tale, "De 'Tiro Largo,'" seems to have furnished the author with the embryo of the novel.[9]

A plague of locusts descends upon the land in both "Saucedo" (*Horizontes y bocacalles*[10]) and *La luna se hizo con agua*,[11] a device so natural in fiction of the region, being so frequently recurring a phenomenon in life, that it is hardly worthy of remark here; it is cited as a contributory fact only. In the novel just mentioned a youthful writer is said to have produced a short story under the title "L'Appassionata." Amorim himself includes in his first series of *cuentos* a curious little tale with that title; the Beethoven composition becomes an actual personage in the story, resolving the problem created by the egocentric narrator; and the unique flavor of the whole situation, coincidence of title and theme, reminiscent air of the passage in the novel, all combine to convince the reader that Amorim is here indulging in an autobiographical touch. It is not uncommon in his work to find such very personal items indicative of his egoism.

From *Horizontes y bocacalles* two more items have been extracted to play new rôles in *El paisano Aguilar*.[12] The character sketch of "Quemacampos" is inserted to introduce the personage now named "don Cayetano Trinidad," who is more fully developed in the course of the novel; another brief sketch of a rustic type, "Un peón," supplies a subsequent scene in the novel. The *peón* remains unnamed in both original and second appearances, a type never developed into an individual personality.

In the light of the foregoing facts it may be significant that Amorim adds as sub-title to his last published collection of stories, *Historias de amor*,[13] what may be taken as an open declaration of policy: "Fragmentos de novela." Even though he has so far given his public no novel built on these preliminary foundations, he apparently reserves the right to do so if he should choose.

The personal quality of Amorim's work has been mentioned above. More evidence of his egoism is found in several of his titles, as may be seen in one case already cited, his first book of stories to which he gave his own surname as title.[14] He offers in justification a saying which he claims is translated from the Persian: "Todo lo nuestro se llama como nosotros." He might have applied the same notion to his preceding publication, a collection of youthful verse that bears the title *Veinte años*, because its date, 1920, marks the poet's own "twenty years" of life. If he has outgrown these obvious egocentric habits of his youth, he has not completely altered his nature. Interested more in his own intellectual processes than in possibly adverse reaction on the part of his reader, he invents a queer title for another book of stories, *Del 1 al 6*,[15] which, with its suggestion of occult significance, can mystify only momentarily: the title is simply indicative of the contents, stories numbered from one to six.

Titles, however, are at best no more than straws showing the direction of the wind; what is far more important is the result of Amorim's re-use of his own material. Some of the short pieces, interesting in themselves, lack sufficient context for best effect, whereas, smoothly fitted and joined to other material in a larger frame, they become improved through the refurbishing essential to appearing in a new environment as well as through the greater service they perform in contributing to the novel structure. Amorim's constant desire to improve his work stands out not only in the re-use of short pieces but also in the changes made in successive editions of his longer fiction. Examples include *La carreta* from its first edition in 1932 to its more or less definitive version in 1942;[16] and the remark prefacing the third edition of *Tangarupá*: ". . . la cual ha sido aumentado en unas partes y reducida en otras, como su autor creyó conveniente."[17]

If the procedure described may properly be termed "self-plagiarism," then Enrique Amorim's plagiarism of himself has produced considerable contribution to the literature of the Río de la Plata region, and has in part justified the means by the achievement of his end, the attainment of a higher degree of literary artistry.

Washington and Lee University

[All books not otherwise specified are published in Buenos Aires.]

[1] *Amorim*: *Cuentos* (Edit. Pegaso; Montevideo, 1923).

[2] Avril, 1929. Quoted by Amorim, *La carreta* (4a. ed., Librerías Anaconda, 1937), p. 253. (This is the edition used for the present study.) For other information from Parisian journals see pp. 251-53.

[3] *Tangarupá* (*un lugar de la tierra*) (Edit. Claridad, 1925). [Novel and three short stories.]

[4] *La carreta* (*novela de quitanderas y vagabundos*) (Claridad, 1932).

[5] *La carreta* (4a. ed.), p. 236.

[6] *Ibid.*, 236-37.

[7] *Autobiography of William Allen White* (New York: Macmillan, 1946), p. 40.

[8] Club del Libro A. L. A., 1941, pp. 197-207.

[9] *La plaza de las carretas* (Domingo Viau, 1937).

[10] Soc. de Publicaciones El Inca, 1926.

[11] Edit. Claridad, 1944.

[12] Claridad, 1936 (2a. ed.). First published Montevideo, Soc. Amigos del Libro Rioplatense, 1934. The edition here used seems identical with the second, but lacks a number of its own and bears copyright date of 1937. See pp. 31-34 for introduction of don Cayetano (as in sketch), and 56-60 for the *peón*.

[13] Santiago de Chile, Eds. Ercilla, 1938.

[14] *Amorim*. Cf. footnote 1 above.

[15] Montevideo, "Impresora Uruguaya," S. A., 1932.

[16] Edit. Claridad, S. A., 1942. Con ilustraciones de Carybé y Prólogo de Ricardo A. Latcham. (Colección Claridad, No. 51.)

[17] Paris, "Le Livre Libre," 1929.

Mark the Boat

MARK THE BOAT
R. S. Boggs

In the time of the Civil War, some villagers heard the Yankees were coming. They wanted to hide their church bell, fearing the Yankees might melt it down to make bullets; so they took it out in a boat on a nearby lake and dropped it over the side into the water. They marked the spot where they had dropped it on the side of the boat, so they could come back and get it later.

I collected this folktale in Buncombe county, North Carolina, and published it[1] some years ago, and found it was known in Ontario, Canada, among Canadians of British descent.[2] Later I heard the same story told about the bell in the courthouse tower at Hillsboro, North Carolina, where it was told as having actually happened during the Revolutionary War, when Dave Fanning and his Tories raided the town in 1781. Although the story is told with great glee by local wags, more serious citizens of Hillsboro categorically deny such stupidity on the part of their ancestors. I have also heard this tale localized in Chapel Hill, North Carolina.

Despite the localization of this story, it is a folktale rather than a legend, and it is listed in the Aarne-Thompson *Types of the Folktale*[3] in almost the same form: A bell falls into the sea, and a mark is made on the boat rail to indicate where it fell. Aarne-Thompson cite variants of it in the indexes of Finnish and Livonian folktales. Since their work appeared, it has also been cited in an index of tales from the Netherlands.[4] In his *Motif-index of folk-literature*,[5] Thompson also lists our tale, and cites W. A. Clouston's *Book of Noodles* (London, 1888) and various other references to it. Among them, he cites the *Ocean of Story*[6] written by Somadeva, a Brahman of Kashmir who wrote in Sanskrit around 1070 A.D. But Somadeva's fool, while traveling by sea, let a silver vessel fall from his hand into the water, and "took notes on the spot, observing the eddies and other signs in the water . . ." This, although similar, lacks the identifying basis of our tale, which is the marking of the spot on the side of the boat. However, the footnote to this tale is pertinent, for it cited a variant about an Irishman hired by a Yarmouth maltster to assist in loading his ship. As the vessel was about to sail, the Irishman cried, "Captain, I lost your shovel overboard, but I cut a big notch on the rail-fence just where it went down, so you will find it when you return." Tawney adds to this note that he has heard that this story of the Irishman is well known in Kashmir, where the term *nāvi-rakh* ('the mark on the ship') is used to mean "stupidity."

The story is also told of Till Eulenspiegel, who may have been a real figure of fourteenth century Germany. Collections of his pranks have circulated in print ever since the early sixteenth century. M. J. Herskovits[7] has given a conveniently accessible summary of Till's version. Till tricks a man, who thinks he hears the beat of war drums, to join him in raising a false alarm in the city of Schoppenstadt. The burghers feared their beautiful new bell in the courthouse steeple might be captured and melted to make gun barrels. Till advised that it be sunk in the sea. One of the councilmen asked how they would be able to tell where the bell had sunk when they went to recover it. "Come with me," Till answered, "and I will show you how to mark the place." All the men of Schoppenstadt assembled, took down the bell, put it in a boat, rowed a little way out to sea, lowered the bell over the side, and let it sink into the sea. "Now I will show you how to mark the spot," said Till, and he took a knife out of his pocket and cut a notch on the side of the boat. "When you want to raise the bell," said Till, "you need only to row out here again, and you will find it right under the notch in the side of the boat."

Herskovits says this story is also heard in Brazil, where stories that parallel many moron tales are told to make sport of the Portuguese; and, although he cites no source, he tells the story from Brazil as follows. João and Manoel were out fishing and found a spot where the catch was especially good. "Be sure and mark the spot, so we can come here tomorrow," said João. Manoel took a piece of chalk from his pocket and made a large "X" on the side of the boat. As they were rowing in, João asked, "Did you mark the spot carefully?" "Yes, see the cross on the side of the boat." "You fool!" João retorted. "Don't you know we'll have a different boat tomorrow?"

In the early 1940's a type of tale flourished in the U. S. A. which was known as the "moron" story. Tales of this kind proved to be a passing fad, and disappeared almost as quickly as they appeared. L. J. Davidson published a collection of them, which includes our story.[8] It tells of two morons fishing. They pulled in lots of fish. In the evening, one said, "You'd better mark this place." When they reached the pier, the first one asked, "Did you mark it?" The second one replied, "Yes, I put a cross on the side of the boat just over the fishing hole." "You fool!" retorted the first. "How do we know that we'll get this boat tomorrow?"

And so we could trace this story on and on, for it appears in the newspapers, it is heard on the radio, and still enjoys a live tradition generally; but the above will suffice to indicate briefly its wide diffusion through time and space. It is of interest because it illustrates clearly and simply some fundamental observations about folklore materials.

The basic idea of this story is obvious and simple, and stories of this type illustrate the possibilities of polygenesis. Thousands of persons riding on a boat have looked up at the sky and felt the illusion that the water must be moving, since they (on the boat) and the sky seemed to be motionless. It is like the telephone poles "passing by" as one sits on a train. Of course, on second thought, one realizes that this is an illusion, but on first thought the impression of a person in a boat that he is not moving may present itself rather vividly. The comic element of our story depends on that illusion, for the absurdity of the story finds acceptance in the first impulse of our illusion; but quickly we recognize that we have been duped, which causes us to laugh, for, curiously, one of the basic precepts of the art of humor is that people will laugh at their stupidity. We might add that the "moron" variant utilizes a second precept of humor: people laugh when they suddenly discover that their minds have been led along one channel while the jester has suddenly jumped to another, leaving them to discover that they have not followed him but are "off the track." When the moron says "You fool!" the listener agrees, because he has just realized the stupidity of marking the boat; but when the teller adds, "How do you know that we'll get this boat tomorrow?" the listener must quickly change the channel of his thought, both to realize his own stupidity in not anticipating this final question and to comprehend that the second moron is as stupid as the first.

With such basic precepts of humor, exploiting the illusion of one's immobility in a boat, to make a variant of our tale does not require any rare inventive genius. The ingredients of our tale are so common that it is quite possible that numerous persons, in different times and places, have blended them together, independently of one another, to produce a story easily recognizable as a variant. Thus, although this story has doubtless spread by diffusion among a multitude of less imaginative informants, it is also quite possible that it may have sprung up independently in a number of different places in different times.

This story also illustrates how a folktale may acquire localizing elements which give it the appearance of a legend. Such elements constitute an integral part of the nature of a legend, but not of a folktale. A legend may vary the names of its persons, the time and place of its action, and other localizing elements; but its character demands that it always be localized somewhere and told about a specific type of person, who is named. The folktale, by nature, is independent of localizing elements. It can say, "Once upon a time, any time you please, in a kingdom, any kingdom you please, there lived a poor boy who finally won the hand of the princess, and their names do not matter." And such is the nature of our tale: any time, in any boat, any person may make his mark on the boat. Its localizing elements may be deleted without affecting the narrative, which indicates that they are superficial and not an integral part of the story. So "Mark the Boat" is a folktale and not a legend, Schoppenstadt or Hillsboro notwithstanding, for the folktale often adorns itself with localizing elements, to stimulate local interest, but it can shed such elements, in favor of others, or do without them. This independence of localizing elements contributes much to the universality of the folktale, which can make itself at home anywhere, and in any time. It is at home in all ages, in all lands, and among all classes of people. Its appeal is universal, hence it comes as near to the concept of "classic" as any artistic form, erudite or folkloric.

Our tale also illustrates something of the relationship between the "popular" and folklore. Folklore is popular, and has been for a long time, long enough to have acquired tradition. But all that is popular is not folklore, for, although some things which are popular today may survive and in time become folklore, most things which are popular today will become covered with the dust of forgetfullness before they have time to acquire the traditional character that comes from being handed down from generation to generation. To separate transient fads and styles from stable folklore is often easy, though we are sometimes blinded by the intense popularity of contemporary passing fads. But fads often pick up traditional materials from folklore and mold them to the particular form which characterizes the fad. In such cases, separation may become more difficult, although, if one knows the folklore materials concerned and the form of the fad, it should be easy to distinguish the one from the other. The form of the moron story was a popular fad in the early 1940's. Then, as a form, its popularity faded, and with it went much of the material that was molded in this form. But "Mark the Boat" was a folktale long before the moron story was invented, and it still lives as a folktale. It was incorporated into the moron story form, and lived and died, as a moron story, with that form; but this was merely a passing phase of its life, which appears to have had little effect on its continuous life as a folktale.

The University of North Carolina

[1] *Journal of American Folklore 1934*, XLVII, 302, no. 20.
[2] F. W. Waugh, *Journal of American Folklore 1918*, XXXI, 78.
[3] Helsinki, Finland, 1928 (Folklore Fellows Communications, no. 74), p. 164, tale type 1278.
[4] J. R. W. Sinninghe, *Katalog der niederländischen Märchen-, Ursprungssagen-, Sagen- und Legendenvarianten*, Helsinki, 1943 (Folklore Fellows Communications no. 132), also under no. 1278.
[5] Helsinki, 1934 (Folklore Fellows Communications, no. 109), IV, 174, no. J 1922.1.
[6] Tawney-Penzer ed. (London, 1926), V, 92-93, no. 114.
[7] *Man and His Works* (New York, 1948), pp. 423-24.
[8] *Southern Folklore Quarterly*, VII (1943), 101.

A Possible Source for Hugo's "Three Ages of Poetry"

A POSSIBLE SOURCE FOR HUGO'S "THREE AGES OF POETRY"

John A. Downs

> "... la poésie a trois âges...."
> —*Préface de Cromwell*

All students of French Literature are familiar with that part of the *Préface de Cromwell* in which Hugo writes a sort of universal history of poetry, dividing it into three parts: lyric, epic, and dramatic. That this division might be based less on sound literary history than on Hugo's imagination was suggested by Rémusat in his review of *Cromwell* in the *Globe* for January 26, 1828.[1] Emile Faguet also found Hugo's idea of writing a universal history of poetry in a few dramatic paragraphs somewhat extravagant, but he excused this extravagance by attributing it to the poet's youth, and to the spirit of the times.

> Ce dessin s'explique très naturellement par l'âge de l'auteur: on a fréquemment à cet âge le goût des aperçus très généraux et des théories qui remontent aux époques les plus lointaines; ensuite par l'esprit du temps: la philosophie de l'histoire date de cette époque.[2]

Souriau suggests that the idea for the three ages of poetry might possibly have been found by Hugo in Mme de Staël's *De la Littérature*, though he offers no evidence to support this suggestion. The small credence which Souriau lends to his own suggestion may be gathered from the wording of his statement:

> Peut-être tout le début de la *Préface* sur les origines des genres, et leur rapport avec les modifications sociales, est-il en partie un emprunt à Mme de Staël; Victor Hugo a voulu lui aussi faire son discours sur l'histoire universelle des littératures; et si le point de vue change quelque peu, le point de départ est le même.[3]

Obviously, Souriau is far from convinced that Hugo was actually influenced by Mme de Staël when he sketched his three ages of poetry. However, in so far as I have been able to determine, Souriau is the only critic who has suggested a possible source for Hugo's ideas on the three divisions of poetry.

In 1771 there was published in Leipzig the first volume of the *Allgemeine Theorie der Schönen Künste* by the Swiss Johann Georg Sulzer.[4] Two years later the second volume appeared, also in Leipzig. This work, on which Bodmer collaborated, was a sort of dictionary of the fine arts, consisting of a series of essays, alphabetically arranged, on the principles of esthetics upon which the fine arts are based.

That the *Allgemeine Theorie* was immediately known, and to some extent popular, in France is evidenced by the fact that several of the essays from it were translated into French and published in the four-volume *Supplément* to the *Encyclopédie*, of which the first volume appeared in 1776. In the article "Poésie (arts de la parole)," which appeared in volume IV (1777) of the *Supplément*, Sulzer traces the history of Greek poetry. It is in this article that Sulzer establishes a possible prototype for Hugo's division of poetry into the three ages: lyric, epic, and dramatic.

The first part of Sulzer's article is given to the distinction between poetry and elocution, and need not concern us here. Having made this distinction, Sulzer then writes a brief historical sketch of Greek poetry. He prefaces his sketch with this statement:

> La véritable histoire de la poésie chez un seul peuple serait incontestablement l'histoire de ce même art chez tous les autres, et ferait sans contredit une partie intéressante de l'histoire universelle du genre humain: mais elle n'existe nulle part.[5]

Sulzer says, in effect, that all poetry has a common history—that what he writes of the history of Greek poetry is equally true of all other poetry. By implication, at least, Sulzer's theory is identical with what Hugo is to say in 1827. Hugo states his opinion as follows:

> Qu'on examine une littérature en particulier, ou toutes les littératures en masse, on arrivera toujours au même fait . . .[6]

Greek poetry, according to Sulzer, may be divided into four periods, which correspond to the successive stages through which Greek society has passed, and to the form of poetry which each successive stage produced. It will be noted that Sulzer distinguishes four periods of society and, consequently, four ages of poetry. However, Sulzer's first two periods correspond, in general, to the primitive, lyric stage with which Hugo begins his *Préface*. A comparison of Sulzer's theory of the origin of poetry with Hugo's description of the poetry of the "temps primitifs" shows a correspondence of ideas, if not of phraseology.

> *Sulzer*
> Dans le cours du premier période de temps, sur lequel il ne nous reste aucune tradition, la poésie commençait à germer imperceptiblement par des sentences proverbiales, ou par des démonstrations de quelque passion agitée qu'on annonçait d'une manière fort succincte, et qu'on chantait en dansant. Ce n'était point encore un art . . .[7]
> *Hugo*
> Aux temps primitifs, quand l'homme s'éveille dans un monde qui

vient de naître, la poésie s'éveille avec lui. En présence des merveilles qui l'environnent sa première parole n'est qu'un hymne.[8]

It is in the close of the first, and more primitive, period that Sulzer finds in poetry the *"traces"* of the three major types which, according to him, constitute the "espèces principales" of poetry.

> Il est vraisemblable que, dès ce temps-là, les tentatives poétiques, renfermaient des indices du caractère différent des trois espèces principales de poésie lyrique, épique et dramatique ... La poésie lyrique paraît naturellement devoir être la plus ancienne, puisqu'elle doit son origine à l'essor des passions tumultueuses.[9]

Hugo's theory on this point closely resembles that of Sulzer. The similarity may be clearly seen by comparing the following passage from the *Préface* with the one quoted above from Sulzer:

> ... c'est que nous n'avons aucunement prétendu assigner aux trois époques de la poésie un domaine exclusif, mais seulement fixer leur caractère dominant. La Bible, ce divin monument lyrique, renferme ... une épopée et un drame en germe, les *Rois* et *Job*. On sent dans tous les poèmes homériques un reste de poésie lyrique et un commencement de poésie dramatique.[10]

Sulzer detects in the lyric poetry of his first two periods a resemblance to the poetry of the Old Testament, and adds that some scholars have found in the primitive poetry of the first of these periods a similarity to "l'histoire que Moïse a donné aux premiers habitants de la terre ..."[11] The poets of the second period, he says, "ont quelque conformité avec les prophètes juifs."[12] Certainly Hugo, if he read Sulzer's article, could have found here the suggestion which caused him to select the Bible as the example of the poetry of the lyric age.

The third period of poetry which Sulzer distinguishes corresponds, in general, to Hugo's epic age of poetry. While it is implicit throughout Sulzer's article that each successive stage of poetry develops out of a corresponding stage in human society, this idea is more specifically stated in the discussion of the origin of epic poetry.

> Le troisième période de la poésie est celui où l'on commence à la regarder comme un art dont la profession faisait un état dans la société ...; alors les poètes ou chantres furent tels en titre d'office ... C'étaient des chantres qu'on appelait et qu'on salariait pour vivre à la cour des princes qui étaient les chefs des petites sociétés d'alors; ... leurs chansoms étaient allégoriques et roulaient sur l'histoire des dieux

et sur les exploits des héros . . . C'est à la fin de ce période . . . que nous plaçons Homère.¹³

The social background which Hugo describes for his epic age is more colorfully portrayed, but the principle that the epic is the outgrowth of a specific social *milieu* is the same in both Sulzer and Hugo. It is interesting to compare Hugo's highly imaginative reconstruction of the epic age with the passage just quoted from Sulzer.

> Cependant les nations commencent à être serrées sur le globe . . . Elles se gênent et se froissent; de là les migrations de peuples, les voyages. La poésie reflète ces grands événements . . . Elle devient épique, elle enfante Homère.¹⁴

Sulzer attributes the advent of the fourth period of Greek poetry to the abolition of the tyranny of the monarchy in most of the states of Greece. The removal of restraint and the development of a greater sense of liberty and equality made it possible for men like Aeschylus, Sophocles, and Euripides to carry poetry to its highest degree of perfection.

> Tant que la Grèce a joui de sa liberté, et que les beaux génies qu'elle produisait ont pu donner l'essor à leurs idées et à leurs sentiments, la poésie s'est soutenue dans ce degré d'élévation qui lui donne la prééminence sur tous les autres arts.¹⁵

This idea that freedom from restraint of rules and from censorship is essential to the dramatist forms the theme of the *Préface*, and is a *sine qua non* which Hugo establishes for the success of dramatic composition. That Hugo would have concurred with Sulzer in this opinion is beyond question.

Since Sulzer bases his theory of a universal history of poetry solely on what he observes in Greek drama, he does not, of course, touch on the advent of Christianity, which, according to Hugo, is the most important influence in the development of the dramatic age of poetry. Sulzer does, however, in his article, sketch the outline of the three ages of poetry, identifies them as lyric, epic, and dramatic, and attributes their development to the social conditions existing during the several periods of Greek culture.

It has been established by both Etienne[16] and Sister O'Connor[17] that Hugo had consulted the *Encyclopédie* as early as 1823. The publication in the *Supplément* of the articles from Sulzer's *Allgemeine Theorie* offered Hugo an opportunity to read Sulzer's work which he would not otherwise have had, since by his own admission he did not read German.[18] Moreover, Hugo's enthusiasm for Germany and German literature was already well-developed by 1827. A treatise on poetry written in German by one who had known Klopstock, Goethe, and Bodmer, as had Sulzer, could hardly have failed to attract Hugo's attention.

It is not always easy to trace Hugo's ideas to their sources. His *Correspondance* contains almost no references to his readings, except for an occasional remark about the work of Chateaubriand. More often than not he completely transformed by his vivid imagination the ideas which he received from others, and assimilated them so completely that their original identity is lost.[19] The "écho sonore" is usually magnified to such an extent that the timbre of the original sound is not identifiable. Sulzer's article on poetry contains the essential ideas of Hugo's "three ages of poetry" and offers a possible source which Hugo might well have used as a point of a departure for his *Préface de Cromwell*.

The University of Georgia

[1] In speaking of the introductory part of the *Préface*, in which Hugo makes the distinction of the three ages of poetry, Rémusat says: "M. Hugo a des vues; les idées ne lui manquent pas, mais il les accueille avec trop peu de sévérité. Lorsqu'il raisonne on dirait encore qu'il imagine." Cited by Des Granges, *La Presse littéraire sous la Restauration*: 1815-1830 (Paris, 1907), p. 350, note.

[2] "Le Romantisme en 1827," *Bull. hébdomadaire des cours et conférences*, 6 déc., 1894. Cited by M. Souriau, éd., *La préface de Cromwell* (Paris, 1897), p. 3, note.

[3] M. Souriau, éd., *La Préface de Cromwell* (Paris, 1897), p.36.

[4] Sulzer was born at Winterthur, Switzerland, 16 Oct. 1720. He was sent to Zurich to study theology, but was attracted instead to natural sciences. He was a pupil of both Gessner and Haller, who strongly influences Sulzer's ideas on scientific investigation. His interest in the literary and esthetic discussions of the period was aroused by Bodmer, for whom he had great admiration. In 1743 Sulzer left Switzerland and went to Prussia. He spent a short time at Magdeburg, where he was closely associated with Klopstock with whom he later made an extended trip to Switzerland. In 1750 Sulzer was made a member of the Royal Academy of Berlin, an honor which he probably owed in part to his ability to please Frederick by speaking and writing excellent French. He died in Berlin in 1779. For a discussion of Sulzer's work see: Anna Tumarkin, *Der Asthetiker Johann Georg Sulzer* (Leipzig, 1933), and G. de Reynolds, *Histoire littéraire de la Suisse au 18ième siècle* (Lausanne, 1912), II, 194-219.

[5] *Supplément à L'Encyclopédie ou Dictionnaire raisonné des sciences, des arts et des métiers* (Paris, 1776), IV, 442.

[6] *La préface de Cromwell*, p. 215.

[7] *Supplément à l'Encyclopédie*, IV, 442.

[8] *Op. cit.*, p. 176.

[9] *Supplément à l'Encyclopédie*, IV, 442.

[10] *Op. cit.*, p. 217.

[11] *Supplément à l'Encyclopédie*, IV, 442.

[12] *Ibid.*, IV, 442.
[13] *Ibid.*
[14] *Op. cit.*, p. 179.
[15] *Supplément à Encyclopédie*, IV, 443.
[16] Servais Etienne, *Les Sources de "Bug Jargal"* (Brussels, 1923).
[17] Sister Mary Irene O'Connor, *A Study of the Sources of "Han d'Islande" and their Significance in the Literary Development of Victor Hugo* (Washington, D. C.: Catholic University Press of America, 1942).
[18] Souriau, éd., *La préface de Cromwell*, p. 23.
[19] This observation is borne out, I believe, by the fact that Souriau rarely cites specific sources for any of Hugo's ideas.

Lucretius and *Micromegas*

LUCRETIUS AND *MICROMEGAS*
Alfred G. Engstrom

Voltaire's Micromégas and his dwarf giant from Saturn are clearly related to Swift's Gulliver and to Rabelais' Gargantua and Pantagruel. But Voltaire introduces elements that differentiate his giants quite sharply from those of Swift and Rabelais.

Gulliver (among the Lilliputians) and Gargantua are huge in proportion to the men and women about them—yet they do not extend beyond the reach of normal vision, their lives are not of staggering length, and their habits remain human.[1] The giants of Brobdingnag are only about twelve times as tall as ordinary men and lead relatively normal, human lives. Voltaire's Micromégas and his dwarf from Saturn, on the contrary, overwhelm us with their established physical proportions, their longevity, and their unnatural behavior.

Micromégas is about twenty-four miles high, and the dwarf towers over a mile above the ground.[2] When the two come to earth and reach the Mediterranean and the great Ocean, they wade through with the greatest ease: "Le nain n'en avait eu jamais qu'à mi-jambe, et à peine l'autre avait-il mouillé son talon."[3] This is beyond the powers of the men of Brobdingnag and far more than Gulliver could have undertaken for all his walking about in the waters between Blefuscu and Lilliput. Voltaire's are unearthly giants and exceed all natural imaginings.

However much Gulliver or the giants of Brobodingnag or Gargantua or Pantagruel may eat, it is always the natural food of mankind, so that the illusion of giant *human* beings is never lost. Not so with Micromégas and the dwarf from Saturn. For some reason they enjoy a quite unnatural repast. Mountains are uprooted to satisfy their hunger: "Après s'être reposés quelque temps, ils mangèrent à leur déjeuner deux montagnes, que leurs gens leur apprêtèrent assez proprement."[4]

We learn that these unearthly creatures live unbelievably long lives—the dwarf from Saturn having a life-expectancy of about 15,000 years and Micromégas himself seven hundred times longer or about 10,500,000 years.[5]

In none of these particulars do Voltaire's giants remind us very closely of the giant heroes of Swift or Rabelais. But there is a passage in the *De rerum natura* of Lucretius that may be pertinent here.[6] It would seem to contain germinal ideas for the particularities cited above in which Voltaire's giants differ from those of his famous predecessors. Lucretius is considering what might occur if something could arise out of nothing. After citing several possibilities, he continues his fantastic speculations as follows:

> denique cur homines tantos natura parare
> non potuit, pedibus qui pontum per vada possent
> transire et magnos manibus divellere montis
> multaque vivendo vitalia vincere saecla . . .[7]

> [Again, why could not nature produce men so large that they could wade through the deep sea as a ford and tear asunder great mountains with their hands and outlive many generations of life . . .]

The passage stands out sharply from the adjacent text in the *De rerum natura*. Its suggestion is one to shock the imagination of a *conteur* like Voltaire. It may even have provided him with the first vivid inspiration for bringing his overwhelming giants to our little earth.

The University of North Carolina

[1] Rabelais' giants expand unexpectedly on many occasions (*e.g.*, in Chapter 37 of Book I where Gargantua uses a comb "qui estoit grand de cent cannes" —nearly two hundred meters in length [Cf. Abel Lefranc, éd., *Oeuvres de François Rabelais* (Paris: Champion, 1913), II, 317, note 8.]—and in the fantastic Chapter 32 of Book II in which the author himself pretends to have spent four happy months on top of one of Pantagruel's teeth and discovered twenty-five inhabited kingdoms in his hero's mouth). But ordinarily the two gigantic heroes move among the rest of mankind on terms of relative equality— talking, playing, eating, and drinking in rather ordinary fashion. Exaggeration of their size, their appetites, or their excretions occurs for comic effects or in various sudden flights of Rabelaisian exuberance.—In *Gulliver*, the *struldbrugs* live forever; but they are ghastly creatures and do not occupy a central place in the narrative.

[2] *Oeuvres complètes de Voltaire* (nouvelle édition, Paris, 1877-83), XXI, 105, 107.

[3] *Ibid.*, p. 112.

[4] *Ibid.*

[5] *Ibid.*, p. 109.

[6] Voltaire was undoubtedly thoroughly familiar with the *De rerum natura* when he wrote *Micromégas* (1752). He refers to Lucretius in *Le temple du goût*, 1733 (*Ouvres complètes*, VIII, 589), and in the dedicatory epistle to *Alzire* (1736) he gives a translation of eight lines from Book II of the *De rerum natura* (*ibid.*, III, 376). At the court of Frederick II he must have found a real enthusiast in the king, "qui apporte aux idées de Lucrèce une adhésion entière" (C.-A. Fusil, "Lucrèce et les philosophes du XVIIIe siècle," *RHLF*, 35 [1928], 207). Later, in 1759, Voltaire himself was even considering a verse translation of the third "canto" of Lucretius' poem (*Oeuvres complètes*, XL, 193).

[7] Lucretius, *De rerum natura* (The Loeb Classical Library ed.; Cambridge, Mass. and London, 1943), Book I, 199-202.

A Note on Old French *bliaut*

A NOTE ON OLD FRENCH *BLIAUT*
Rosalyn Gardner

The earliest known occurrence of a form of *blialt* or *bliaut* "frock, smock, or the material from which they are made" is in the *Chanson de Roland* in the latter part of the eleventh century.

> E li quens en fut molt angoissables,
> De son col gietet ses grandes pels de martre
> Ed est remés en son *blialt* de palie. (vv. 301-303)[1]

The word appears in other Romance languages:

Provençal *blial, blidal, bliau, brizaut*

> El cors graile, delgat a fresc e lis
> Trop ben estan en *bliau*. (Bertrand de Born, *Ges de disnar*)

> Sabon far un *blizaut*
> O autre vestir benestan. (R. Vidal de Bezaudun, *Abrils issi'*)

> Mantel a *blial* de violas
> E sobrecot de rosas. (P. Guillem de Tolosa, *Lai on cobra*)

Spanish *brial*

> Tras una viga lagar—metios' con grant pavor;
> el manto e el *brial*—todo suzio lo sacó. (*Poema del Cid*)[2]

Portuguese *brial*

> Ela vesteu logo hun *brial* moy nobre, que era de
> hun moy fremoso paño ... (*Amores de Breçaida*).[3]

From the French it penetrated the Germanic languages: Middle Low German *bliant, blyant*; Middle English *bleaunt*; Middle High German *blîalt, blîat*. Mediaeval Latin apparently borrowed it from Romance as *blialdus, bliaudus*, and even *blisaudus* from the Provençal.

The origin of the word is given as unknown by Bloch,[4] Dauzat,[5] and Gamillscheg.[6] The *FEW*[7] postulates *blidalt* of uncertain origin: "Der ursprung des nur gallorom. typus *blidalt* ist unbekannt." Meyer-Lübke, in the *REW*,[8] also gives *blidalt* and suggests a possible Oriental origin: "Wohl orientalisch?" The *blidalt* is a logical base and could account for any Romance form that we have, including Provençal *blizaut*. But it is hardly likely that the word is of Arabic derivation, as the final *-lt* is not a good Oriental pattern. The consonantal clusters would suggest rather a Germanic origin.

Our problem, therefore, is to indicate a possible Germanic equivalent of *blidalt* in the late Old High German period, since *bliaut* occurs in Old French earlier than the Middle High German period. Old Teutonic **bregdan* "to pull, to twitch, to pull quickly hither and thither, to move suddenly to and fro" gave Old High German *brettan* which appeared in Middle High German as *briten* "to weave" (cf. English *braid*).[9] A parallel substantive development of **bregdan* with the addition of the instrumental *-ila* suffix[10] was in Old High German *brittil*,[11] Middle High German *britel, brîdel* "bridle."[12] A primary meaning in late Old High German of *brittil* (or *brîdel*) should have been "shuttle" or "weaving instrument." A verbal derivative (OHG [*gi-*]*brittolon*,[13] late OHG *britelen* or *bridelen*) must consequently have had an early sense similar to that of the simple verb *brettan* (MHG *briten*), "to weave." The situation is a little confused because the surviving MHG *britelen* or *bridelen* has only the meaning of "to bridle, to curb," and the primary sense of "to weave" seems to be lost in the extant literature. We are assuming, however, that the verb *britelen* "to weave" existed. The close relationship between the two meanings is evident. *Britel, brîdel* "bridle" and *briten* "to weave" have a common root meaning of "to pull back and forth." The *New English Dictionary* gives as one meaning of *bridle* "the cord or other work which strengthens or tightens the sides of a net." Alexander Neckham, in his Latin vocabulary, composed in the 12th century, likens a weaver to the driver of a horse: "A weaver is a horseman on *terra firma* who leans upon two stirrups and who gives rein constantly to the horse, content with a short journey..."[14]

With the above in mind, we suggest that the past participle of *britelen, bridelen* would be *britelt* or *bridelt* "woven," which could easily become **blidalt*, then *blialt* "a tunic or the material from which it is woven."

The University of North Carolina

---

[1] *La Chanson de Roland*, ed. Rosalyn Gardner, W. S. Woods, and H. H. Hilton, Jr. (Boston: Ginn, 1942).

[2] *Poema del Cid*, ed. Victor R. B. Oelschläger (New Orleans: Newcomb College and Tulane University, 1948), vv. 2290-91.

[3] *Amores de Breçaida* in *Crestomatia arcaica*, ed. José Joaquim Nunes (3rd ed.; Lisbon: Livraria Clássica Editora, Teixeira, 1943), p. 117.

[4] O. Bloch, *Dictionnaire étymologique de la langue française*, Vol. I (Paris: Les Presses Universitaires de France, 1932).

[6] A. Dauzat, *Dictionnaire étymologique de la langue française* (Paris: Larousse, 1938).

[6] E. Gamillscheg, *Etymologisches Wörterbuch der französischen Sprache* (Heidelberg: Carl Winter, 1928).

[7] W. von Wartburg, *Französisches etymologisches Wörterbuch*, Vol. I (Bonn: F. Klopp, 1928).

[8] W. Meyer-Lübke, *Romanisches etymologisches Wörterbuch* (3rd ed.; Heidelberg: Carl Winter, 1935), § 1169.

[9] *A New English Dictionary on Historical Principles*, Vol. I, ed. J. A. H. Murray (Oxford: The Clarendon Press, 1888); and Georg F. Benecke and Wilhelm Müller, *Mittelhochdeutsches Wörterbuch*, Vol. I (Leipzig: S. Hirzel, 1854).

[10] Friedrich Kluge, *Nominale Stammbildungslehre der altgermanischen Dialekte* (3rd ed.; Halle: Niemeyer, 1926), § 90.

[11] E. G. Graff, *Althochdeutscher Sprachschatz oder Wörterbuch der althochdeutschen Sprache*, Vol. III (Berlin: Nikolaischen Buchhandlung, 1837), p. 299.

[12] *Mittelhochdeutsches Wörterbuch*, Vol. I.

[13] Graff, *op. cit.*, p. 299.

[14] Thomas Wright, ed., *A Volume of Vocabularies* (Privately printed, 1857), p. 106.

Romance Languages in North Carolina, 1909-1949

ROMANCE LANGUAGES IN NORTH CAROLINA, 1909-1949

Hugo Giduz

A precise evaluation of the factors which have promoted the study of Romance Languages during the past fifty years in the University of North Carolina and in the high schools of the state is of course impossible. However, one may consider the status of such study in 1909, the year in which Mr. Dey began his term as head of the Department of Romance Languages at the University, and compare it with the situation at present—1949.

In 1909, the staff of the Department of Romance Languages and Literatures consisted of three persons: Professor W. M. Dey, head of the department; Assistant Professor Oliver Towles; and Instructor Adolphe Vermont. There were six courses in French listed in the catalogue. In addition to his French courses, Mr. Dey taught three Spanish courses. Mr. Vermont gave one elementary course in Italian and was the first President of Le Cercle Français, which was founded in 1907.

The following year, 1908, Mr. Luther Wood Parker was the President, and Mr. Vermont the Secretary of the Cercle. In 1909, Mr. Dey was the President, and Mr. Vermont was made Permanent Secretary.

In the 1910-1911 catalogue we find the notation: "Pronunciation is taught by the Phonetic Method." In 1914-1915, four courses were added to the offerings of the department. During the same year there is a statement that "the Direct Method of Instruction is used." Two years later the catalogue states that "the Direct Method is no longer in use, but special attention is given to pronunciation."

By 1921-1922 the departmental staff numbered thirteen, and several courses were added in both French and Spanish, as well as five courses in Italian, given by Professor Howard R. Huse, and one course in Portuguese, given by Professor Sturgis E. Leavitt. Le Cercle Français was no longer headed by faculty members, but by students. In 1922-1923, El Centro Hispano was organized.

At this time the teaching staff of the department had fifteen faculty members and two teaching fellows. The offerings on both the undergraduate and the graduate level were increased. Both the number of faculty members and the course offerings continued to increase almost every year, until by 1943-1944 there were fifty-one men teaching in the department. This number included four teaching fellows, two research assistants and two assistants. The number of courses listed in the catalogue had risen to fifty-seven in French, forty-six in Spanish, six in Italian and three in Portuguese. In 1949, the last year during which Mr. Dey was Head of the Department, the staff consisted of fifty-nine persons, including three women teaching fellows and one research assistant. The course offerings numbered forty-seven in French, thirty-six in Spanish, five in Portuguese and eight in Italian.

There is no report available of the number of students in the Romance Languages Department for 1909-1910. The catalogue shows that there were 252 students enrolled in the department in 1910-1911. The number of students registered for the Romance Languages has increased fairly consistently until now in 1949 there are 2216 studying French, Spanish, Portuguese, and Italian.

A survey of the growth of the study of the Romance Languages in the high schools of the state reveals some equally interesting statistics. In 1909 there were 559 high school students taking French; 9,785 were studying Latin; 100 were registered in Greek. Spanish was not taught at this time. By 1935-1936 the enrollment in French had risen to 38,674; 755 were then registered in Spanish; Latin had 16,161 students; and Greek was no longer offered. This made a total of 55,590 who were studying foreign languages.

The May, 1949, issue of the North Carolina Public School Bulletin shows that the total number of students taking French was only 22,853; 5,200 were in Spanish; and Latin had dropped to 9,253. A total of no more than 37,306 high school students were enrolled in foreign language study that year. It is interesting to note that of this number 8,392 were Negroes. The decrease is more noteworthy when one considers that of a total high school enrollment of 12,031 in 1909, 10,734 were taking foreign language courses, while in 1949, with a total enrollment of 167,098, only 37,306 were in languages courses! In other words, 89% of the high school students were studying foreign languages in 1909, whereas in 1949 only about 22% were doing so.

To return to another phase of foreign language activity, let us consider the matter of graduate degrees in the University from 1909-1949.

One A.M. was granted in French in 1908, the year before Mr. Dey took over the duties as Head of the Romance Languages Department. Not until 1912 was another A.M. granted. It was 1924 before any more such degrees were awarded, and in that year there were seven. After that at least one degree of Master of Arts was awarded each year. In 1938 there were fourteen—the largest number in the history of the department. A total of 160 Master's degrees had been awarded through 1949.

The first doctoral degree from the department was awarded in 1928. There was at least one Ph.D. awarded almost every year thereafter; in 1948 there were eight. Through 1949, the total number of Ph.D.'s was forty-nine. Thus the total number of graduate degrees granted during the time that Mr. Dey was head of the department is 208.

If we consider, in addition to these graduate degrees, the undergraduates who received their A.B.'s with a major in Romance Languages, many of whom went out to teach in the high schools, we see that the influence of the Department has been very great. Not only has this influence made itself felt in North Carolina, but in all the Southern states and elsewhere, for in many institutions graduates of this department of Romance Languages may be found among the faculty members.

The University of North Carolina

A Note on the Word *Fauve*
In Old French

A NOTE ON THE WORD *FAUVE* IN OLD FRENCH
Marion A. Greene

The figure of speech *fauve asnesse* occurs in the *Roman de Renart* and the *Renart Nouvel* with the abstract meaning of "deceit" or "trickery": "molt savez de la fauve annesse"[1]; "Renars qui scet de fauve anesse"[2]; "tout juent de la fauve anesse."[3]

The above usage may serve to throw some light on the hitherto obscure meaning of the tawny mule upon which the hideous damsel rides in the *Conte del Graal*. Is it pure coincidence that her mount is yellowish? It seems more probable that the color in this case has a symbolic meaning closely related to the idea of deceit which is inherent in the adjective *fauve* as indicated above. Holmes, in his discussion of Chrétien's *Conte del Graal*,[4] points out that the tawny mule has a special significance in view of the fact that the word "yellow" does not even appear in the vast index of Louis Ginzberg's *The Legends of the Jews*.[5] This would seem to imply an unfavorable implication of the color in the eyes of the Jews. Holmes further relates the color to the sinful state of the damsel. It appears highly probable that her "fauve" mule represents deceit.

In the *Roman de Fauvel* the animal protagonist is a roan or tawny horse. Here, too, the color evidently denotes the deceitful nature of the beast as well as its reddish-yellow coat.

>   Fauvel lour a trop bien rendu
>   Ce qu'il avoient entendu
>   A vivre ou siecle faussement.[6]

Tilander in his *Lexique du Roman de Renart*[7] defines the verb *fauvoier* as meaning "se moquer de, tromper, égarer," which he says evidently derives from *fauve* used in the sense in which that adjective is employed in the phrase *fauve anesse*. By the Middle French period and possibly before, the adjective is also employed in the phrase *bêtes fauves* to mean "wild animals." Cotgrave so uses it.[8] This meaning may have had its origin in the idea of deceit. That is to say, the term "wild animals" may have referred to those animals who snared their prey by trickery.

The color yellow when used adjectivally has a pejorative meaning and is associated variously with such evils as sickness, punishment, jealously, and cowardice. For example, jaundice is commonly called the "yellow evil." The adjective is regularly allied with certain illnesses such as yellow fever and the yellow plague. Calling a person "yellow" is tantamount to calling him a coward. A yellow flag or sign is the indication of an infectious disease or quarantine. Formerly it was employed as a signal of capital punishment.[9] Shakespeare in his *Winter's Tale* symbolically alludes to jealously through the word yellow: "If thou hast the ordering of the mind, too, mongst all colors no yellow in it."[10] Addison in the *Freeholder* refers to men who hid themselves at the sight of yellow: "When he appear'd in yellow, his great men hid themselves in corners."[11]

Similar popular conceptions of the color yellow must have existed in the mind of the mediaeval French writer. Certainly red was associated with evil during this period. On the mediaeval stage we find Judas, the arch-traitor, and the devil, the embodiment of evil, represented with red hair.[12]

In the expression *fauve anesse* the meaning of the adjective is made doubly clear by the following noun. The ass in the mediaeval bestiaries was presented as an evil and treacherous character. For example, the wild ass in the bestiary of Philippe de Thaün signifies the devil:

> Onager par raisun
> Asne salvage at num.
> . . . .
> Onager signefie
> Diable en ceste vie.[13]

The wild ass in the bestiary of Guillaume de Normandie has the face of a demon.[14]

A French proverb "méchant comme un âne rouge" connotes the wicked nature of the red ass.[15]

Thus, *fauve*, when used with the noun *asnesse*, carries the pejorative meaning associated with the devilish character of the ass. When disassociated from its noun it is probable that the adjective continued to maintain the basic idea of deceit. This necessarily would apply, also, to its diminutives *fauvel* and *fauvelet*.

The Universty of Maryland

---

[1] Ernest Martin, éd., *Roman de Renart* (Strassburg: Trübner, 1882-87), Br. I, 1291.

[2] *Ibid.*, VI, 161.

[3] *Renart Nouvel*, 885.

[4] Urban T. Holmes, Jr., *A New Interpretation of Chrétien's Conte del Graal* (Studies in the Romance Languages and Literatures, No. 8; Chapel Hill: University of North Carolina, 1948).

[5] *Ibid.*, p. 15.

⁶ Studer and Waters, eds., *Historical French Reader, Mediaeval Period* (Oxford: Clarendon Press, 1924), p. 205, ll. 248-50.

⁷ Gunnar Tilander, *Lexique du Roman de Renart* (Göteborg: Elanders Boktryckeri Aktiebolag, 1924), p. 79.

⁸ Randle Cotgrave, *A Dictionarie of the French and English Tongues* (London: Adam Islip, 1611).

⁹ *N. E. D.* (*Oxford*: Clarendon Press, 1928), X, 35.

¹⁰ Act II, sc. 3, l.107.

¹¹ No 10. 60.

¹² Maximilian Rudwin, *The Devil in Legend and Literature* (London: The Open Court Publishing Company, 1931), p. 46.

¹³Emmanuel Walberg, éd., *Le Bestiaire de Philippe de Thaün* (Paris: H. Welter, 1900), p. 68. This was taken from the *Physiologus* and therefore was a current bestiary legend throughout the Middle Ages. Cf. Friedrich Fauchert's *Physiologus* (Strassburg, 1889), p. 36.

¹⁴ Robert Reinsch, ed., *Le Bestiaire, das Thierbuch des normannischen Dichters Guillaume le Clerc* . . . (Leipzig, Reisland, 1892).

¹⁵ Armand-Georges Billandeau, *Recueil de locutions françaises* (Paris: Boyveau et Chevillet, 1930), p. 30.

Charles Peguy et la mystique francaise

CHARLES PÉGUY ET LA MYSTIQUE FRANCAISE

Jacques Hardré

On parle beaucoup de Charles Péguy depuis les dix dernières années. Quelles que soient leurs tendances politiques ou leurs croyances religieuses, les Français d'aujourd'hui s'accordent tous à reconnaître en lui un grand écrivain. A quoi tient cette unanimité? Comment se fait-il que cet homme qui, de son vivant, combattit presque toutes les institutions et tous les partis soit aujourd'hui enseigné en Sorbonne et réclamé comme un des leurs par les hommes de droite et par les hommes de gauche, sans parler de l'Eglise catholique et des anti-cléricaux?

Une explication semble être que dans toute son oeuvre Péguy s'acharne à défendre la mystique contre la politique. Ou plutôt à empêcher que la mystique ne dégénère en politique. Or, il y a plusieurs types de mystiques: la républicaine, la royaliste, la socialiste, la chrétienne. Comme il y a plusieurs types de politiques: la républicaine, la royaliste, la socialiste, et la chrétienne. Les mystiques s'entendent toujours, ce sont les politiques qui se combattent. Pour Péguy, et cela l'explique en grande partie, il n'y a pas de contradictions entre les grands mouvements mystiques. Cette conception se dégage très nettement de celles de ses oeuvres qui traitent de l'Affaire Dreyfus, en premier lieu de celle intitulée *Notre jeunesse*. Dans l'Affaire, Péguy retrouve toutes les mystiques qu'il aime: la mystique juive, représentée par Bernard Lazare, qu'il compare aux anciens prophètes d'Israël; la mystique chrétienne, car les vrais chrétiens étaient, selon lui, du côté de Dreyfus; et, surtout, la mystique française.

Qu'entend-il par cette dernière? Pour bien le comprendre il faut se rappeler qu'il existe en France plusieurs grandes familles spirituelles: la famille spirituelle chrétienne, dont les grandes figures sont Saint Louis, Sainte Jeanne d'Arc et Saint Vincent de Paul; la famille spirituelle démocratique et socialiste, dont les représentants sont Voltaire, Diderot et Jaurès; et finalement la famille spirituelle du traditionalisme français. Cette dernière, lorsqu'elle s'allie à la famille chrétienne représente la tradition monarchique et lorsqu'elle s'allie à la famille démocratique représente la tradition jacobine. Ce qui fait le charme de Péguy c'est justement qu'il unit toutes ces familles dans ce qu'elles ont de plus général et de plus mystique et qu'il donne à cette union la tâche de poursuivre la destinée surnaturelle de la France: celle d'accomplir dans le monde le rêve de la cité de Dieu. Ainsi s'explique que Péguy pouvait être à la fois chrétien, socialiste, et ancienne France. Ainsi s'explique pourquoi, pendant sa vie, il ne pouvait être accepté par aucun groupe et que, mort, il soit accaparé par tous.

L'idée que Péguy se fait de la destinée surnaturelle de la France se trouve dans plusieurs de ses oeuvres poétiques comme *Le mystère des saints innocents*, *Le porche du mystère de la deuxième vertu*, *Les tapisseries* ainsi que dans certaines de ses oeuvres en prose telles que *Notre patrie*, *Notre jeunesse*, *L'argent et L'argent (suite)*. Il serait aisé d'établir la hiérarchie française et la hiérarchie chrétienne selon Péguy (car pour lui les deux s'enchevêtrent et se confondent presque) et de les représenter dans un de ces tableaux moyenâgeux où le Ciel et la Terre figurent sur un même plan. Au milieu serait Dieu le Père, vénérable mais familier, avec un soupçon de malice paysanne dans le regard. Groupés autour de lui se tiendraient la Vierge Marie, Jésus, et "l'aïeule aux longs cheveux," notre mère Eve. Auprès d'eux se trouveraient les Saints parmi lesquels les plus près de la Vierge seraient Saint-Louis, Sainte Geneviève, et Sainte Jeanne d'Arc. Les serrant de près il y aurait les "témoins préférés," les "meilleurs soldats," les "meilleurs serviteurs" de Dieu: le peuple français. Quant au paysage qui formerait le fond de ce tableau, ce serait:

> ". . . . ces plaines et ces vallonnements de France
> Qui sont plus beaux que tout."

> "Le pays des beaux blés et des encadrements,
> Le pays de la grappe et des ruissellements
> Le pays de genêts, de bruyères, de lande."

où figureraient:

> ". . . Paris et Reims et Rouen et des cathédrales qui sont mes propres palais et mes propres châteaux, Si beaux que je les garderai dans le ciel."

(C'est Dieu qui parle.)

Remarquons que Péguy, qui se disait un homme du quinzième siècle, avait effectivement la foi naïve du Moyen Age que l'on retrouve, par exemple, chez Villon. Lorsqu'il fait parler Dieu c'est en un Dieu paternel qui s'intéresse directement aux affaires des Ses créatures, qui s'étonne parfois de ce qu'Il a créé:

> "Ce qui m'étonne, dit Dieu, c'est l'espérance.
> Et je n'en reviens pas."

C'est un Dieu qui connaît dans les moindres détails les menus travaux des paysans et des artisans. Et c'est un Dieu qui a une préférence toute particulière pour le peuple français:

> "C'est embêtant, dit Dieu, Quand il n'y aura plus ces Français,
> Il y a des choses que je fais, il n'y aura plus personne pour les comprendre."

Il est intéressant de noter quelles sont les qualités que Dieu aime chez les Français. En premier lieu, la liberté:

> "Ils ont la liberté dans le sang. Tout ce qu'ils font, ils le font librement.
> Ils sont moins esclaves et plus libres dans le péché même
> Que les autres ne le sont dans leurs exercices. Par eux nous avons goûté,
> Par eux nous avons inventé, par eux nous avons créé
> D'être aimé par des hommes libres."

Ensuite, la gratuité:

> "C'est un peuple, dit Dieu, qui a la gratuité dans le sang. Il donne et
>   ne retient pas.
> Il donne et ne reprend pas.
> . . . . . .
> Et ainsi c'est le peuple qui se conforme le plus littéralement
> Aux paroles de mon fils. Et qui le plus littéralement réalise
> Les paroles de mon fils."

L'intelligence et le labeur:

> "Ils n'ont pas besoin qu'on leur explique vingt fois la même chose.
> Avant qu'on ait fini de parler, ils sont partis.
> Peuple intelligent,
> Avant qu'on ait fini de parler, ils ont compris.
> Peuple laborieux,
> Avant qu'on ait fini de parler, l'oeuvre est faite."

Ce Dieu qui parle ainsi est également le Dieu des batailles. Il n'est donc pas étonnant de l'entendre dire:

> "Peuple soldat, dit Dieu, rien ne vaut le Français dans la bataille.
> (Et ainsi rien ne vaut le Français dans la croisade).
> Ils ne demandent pas toujours des ordres et ils ne demandent pas toujours des explications sur ce qu'il faut faire et sur ce qui va se passer . . . . .
> . . . .
> "Ils se débrouillent tout seuls. Ils comprennent tout seuls. En pleine bataille.
> . . . .
> "Sans déranger le général. Or il y a toujours la bataille, dit Dieu,
> Il y a toujours la croisade.
> Et on est toujours loin du général."

Citons finalement ce passage bien connu:

> "Peuple, les peuples de la terre te disent léger
> Parce que tu es un peuple prompt.
> Les peuples pharisiens te disent léger
> Parce que tu es un peuple vite.
> Tu es arrivé avant que les autres soient partis.
> Mais moi je t'ai pesé, dit Dieu, et je ne t'ai point trouvé léger.
> O peuple inventeur de la cathédrale, je ne t'ai point trouvé léger en foi.
> O peuple inventeur de la croisade, je ne t'ai point trouvé léger en charité.
> Quant à l'espérance, il vaut mieux ne pas en parler, il n'y en a que pour eux.
>
> "Tels sont nos Français, dit Dieu. Ils ne sont pas sans défauts. Il s'en faut. Ils ont même beaucoup de défauts.
> Ils ont plus de défauts que les autres.
> Mais avec tous leurs défauts je les aime encore mieux que les autres avec censément moins de défauts,
> Je les aime comme ils sont . . . . ."

Péguy voit donc dans la race française certaines qualités qui font d'elle, disons-le, la race élue. C'est une race qui a la tâche non de conquérir le monde et d'y imposer ses volontés mais de répandre l'amour de la liberté et de la chrétienté, de la justice et du libéralisme. Il faut bien comprendre cette haute conception de la mystique française afin de saisir toute l'importance de l'Affaire Dreyfus dans la vie de Péguy. Pour lui la France ne pouvait se permettre la moindre tache morale sous peine de déchoir de son rôle spirituel. Voilà ce qui explique sa fureur contre ceux de ses adversaires qui proclamaient que le prestige de l'Armée valait bien une vie sacrifiée. Non, répondait Péguy, rien ne peut excuser, rien ne vaut la moindre injustice, l'impureté la plus infime. Cette intransigeance explique également sa furer contre certains Dreyfusards qui, l'Affaire terminée, se servaient de la mystique dreyfusiste pour arriver à leurs fins politiques. Pour lui, c'était une trahison.

Toutes ces qualités qu'il exalte dans le peuple français, il les trouve incarnées dans celle qui a joué un énorme rôle dans son dévelopement spirituel, dans celle qu'il a nommée:

> La fille la plus sainte après la Sainte Vierge.
> . . . (celle qui) fut et la plus éminente et la plus fidèle et la plus approchée de toutes les imitations de Jésus-Christ,

dans "l'humble bergère," "la fille de Lorraine": Sainte Jeanne d'Arc. Droiture, énergie, bravoure, pureté, voilà ce qui caractérise la Jeanne de Péguy. Une certaine impatience aussi et une intransigeance absolue lorsqu'il s'agit de sa mission. Si l'on ajoute à cela le désir ardent de vaincre le Mal et de réaliser le rêve de Dieu sur Terre, l'on voit combien elle ressemble à l'idée du Français que se fait l'auteur de *Notre patrie*.

De nombreux écrivains ont composé des oeuvres sur la Pucelle. Aucun n'en a parlé comme Péguy et cela se comprend. Ils avaient, elle et lui, tant en commun.

La mystique française de Péguy est donc une mystique d'une très haute portée morale. Tout en reconnaissant les défauts du Français, il loue ses qualités et ceci uniquement dans l'intention de le forcer à se rendre compte de sa mission. C'est une mystique que peu d'étrangers arrivent à comprendre et dont ils ne peuvent s'empêcher de sourire. Mais c'est une mystique qui répond à une aspiration, souvent inconsciente, chez les Français et dans laquelle ils puisent, en temps de crise, un renouveau de courage, une nouvelle source d'espoir.

Serait-ce là la véritable explication de l'actualité de Péguy?

The University of North Carolina

A Troubadour Lesson
In Practical Semantics

A TROUBADOUR LESSON IN PRACTICAL SEMANTICS
Elliott Dow Healy

In his *Provenzalisches Supplement-Wörterbuch,* Emil Levy indicates some dissatisfaction and hesitancy as to the correct definition of Old Provençal *franc*. In particular he is inclined to take issue with Carl Appel, from whose *Provenzalische Chrestomathie* he draws many of the illustrations used in the *Supplement-Wörterbuch*. In his glossary Appel lists only the word *edel* as a translation for Provençal *franc* in all connotations. This Levy feels to be entirely inadequate. For example, considering its interpretation in the following couplet cited by Appel from Raimon Vidal:

> Amiga, dona, franqu'e pura
> Per amor Dieu perdonatz me . . .

he asks rather pointedly, "Sind *franqua* und *pura* synonym? Oder is *edel* zu deuten, wie es Appel nicht nur an dieser, sondern an allen Stellen seiner Chrestomathie thut?"[1] He then proceeds to give no less than thirteen definitions, and examination of well known chrestomathies and anthologies in German, English, French, and Italian permits increasing this number to about twenty-five, even after making allowances for the overlapping which is likely to occur because of the different languages represented. Reducing this list of terms to English for the sake of consistency and comparison, we find the following translations offered for *franc* alone, without considering any of its variants or derivatives: *free, noble, sincere, frank, candid, loyal, faithful, upright, innocent, good, sweet, affable, pure, lofty, exalted, open, emancipated, gratuitous, debonair, friendly, mild, gracious, unrestrained, unruly,* and *unlimited*. Obviously a number of these terms may be classed as near synonyms, but even with this restriction it would be surprising in the extreme if the term *franc* had in the troubadour mind any such vague or generalized meaning as this multiplicity of possible translations would suggest, despite the fact that its origin in an ethnic term placed but little restriction upon its semantic development. On the other hand it is clear from even a cursory examination of troubadour usage that Appel's single definition *edel*, with the basic meaning of *noble*, would not suffice as an adequate translation in numerous instances. It is of interest to note here that Godefroy lists only three meanings for the Old French *franc*: *noble, libre,* and *libérateur*.

There may well be two legitimate points of view toward a matter of this nature. In the first place it is undeniably helpful to a student, or to an anthologist assembling a glossary which will be adequate to the needs of students and non-critical readers, to provide enough definitions in his own language to permit smooth and rhythmic translation. Yet it is also a matter of some concern to render the tribute of exactness, insofar as possible, to the interpretation of the creative thought of the troubadours, the earliest representatives of a cultivated literature in the Romance vernaculars. From the latter point of view it would seem that the general question raised by Levy deserves an answer.

With this thought in mind, the *canso* of Lanfranc Cigala[2] which begins *Tan franc cors de dompn' ai trobat* and which is addressed to a certain N'Ailas de V . . . offers us something more than an amusing play on the word *franc* and its derivatives. It suggests, in effect, a concise if unintentional lesson in practical semantics, for Lanfranc succeeded very well indeed in using *franc* or one of its variants in every one of the twenty lines (two strophes and *tornada*) of which the poem is composed. It goes without saying that he would hardly be able to cover all possible uses of the word in such a whimsical poem of less than normal *canso* length, but nonetheless it is of more than passing interest in its bearing upon what *franc* must have meant in the minds of the troubadours themselves. The poem follows:

I. Tan *franc* cors de dompn' ai trobat
A Villafranca e tan plazen
Qe m'accuilli tan *francamen*
Qe de *franc* m'a sos sers tornat.
Mas *franqeza*, com m'adui a servir,
Qe'm deuria, s'eu era sers, *franqir?*
Qe pros dompna, ab sa *franca* douzor,
Cor d'ome *franc* fai leu son servidor.

II. S'ieu ages ges de *franqetat*
Eu amera son *franc* cors gen,
Mas no ai tan *franc* ardimen
D'entendr'en tan *franc'* amistat;
Mas son *franc* pretz sivals farai auzir
Tan qe mains *francs* farai sers devenir
De lei cui am *francamen* ad honor
Ab fi cor *franc*, mas no en dreit d'amor.

III. Dompna, ia mais no voill *francs* devenir
De vos honrar *francamen* e servir,
Q'eu fora fols, pois ai tan *franc* seignor,
Si *franqetat* demandava maior.[3]

A quick recapitulation shows that *franc* occurs eleven times as an adjective, including its perfectly logical appearance as a part of the place name Villafranca, twice as a concrete noun, and three times in adverbial form. The verb *franqir* appears once, and the abstracts *franqeza* and *franqetat* once and twice respectively. One might therefore expect a fairly representative use of the basic concept involved in a reasonably varied sampling of connotations. Do the italicized words in the above poem have a wide variety of meanings, or may they be limited to those two or three definitions which follow most closely the etymological sense of the term? It will be of interest to examine a translation of Lanfranc's poem for whatever light it may be able to throw upon the question. The following is rendered as literally as is consistent with a wholesome regard for accuracy and apparent meaning, using those English equivalents which seem to fall most logically into the pattern of thought developed by the troubadour:

I. Such a *noble* and so pleasing a figure of a woman have I found at Villafranca, who welcomes me so *nobly* (freely?) that from a *free* man she has changed me into her slave. But *freedom*, since it leads me to serve, should it not, if I were a slave, *free* me? For a worthy lady with her *noble* gentleness easily makes the heart of a *free* man her servant.

II. If I possessed any *freedom* at all, I should love her *noble*, gentle self, but I do not have so *free* an ardor as to hope for such a noble friendship. But I shall at least make known her *noble* worth, so that I shall make many a *free* man become the servant of her whom I love *freely* with honor, with a true, *noble* heart, but not with the right of possession.

III. Lady, never do I wish to be *free* from honoring and serving you *freely*, for I would be a fool, since I have so *noble* a sovereign, if I should demand greater *freedom*.

It is at once apparent that this translation might be improved in smothness, melody, and freshness if some of the varied definitions of *franc* offered by the lexicographers were employed. The purpose, however, in this case is not to present a polished and finished English version of the *canso*, but to seek as accurately as possible to grasp the reality of the poet's thought. The real question, therefore, is whether the above translation is faithful to the intent and purpose of the troubadour, whether it represents the true expression which he desired to achieve. Unfortunately it is hardly possible to answer such a question with any degree of certainty. It is suggested, however, that Lanfranc would hardly have attempted such a poetic *tour de force* unless his skill in the clever juggling of the same word, with substantially the same meanings, would be recognized. Moreover, it may be pointed out that the two basic interpretations used, *noble* and *free*, do no violence to logic, and make excellent sense in every case. This is particularly true in those instances in which *franc* itself is employed. The fact remains that with these two interpretations the poem hangs together as a logical whole. It suggests that for Lanfranc Cigala the Old French and Old Provençal usage of the term were for all practical purposes one and the same, and we may fairly assume that his was a representative troubadour point of view. Obviously there are cases in which other meanings, those of *frank* or *open*, for example, are indicated, but it appears very doubtful that there is any justification at all in the whole body of troubadour verse for the manifold interpretations which the glossaries offer for this particular word.

Louisiana State University

[1] Emil Levy, *Provenzalisches Supplement-Wörterbuch*. (Leipzig: Reisland, 1894-1924), III, 586.

[2] Lanfranc Cigala was a Genoese troubadour, flourishing in the mid-thirteenth century. The *canso* here cited was undoubtedly written as a *tour de force*, but Lanfranc Cigala, despite his Italian origin, was a sufficiently masterful craftsman in the language of his literary adoption to justify confidence in his linguistic accuracy.

[3] Text from MS. H.

The Dominican Rite and the
Judaeo-Christian Theory of the Grail

THE DOMINICAN RITE AND THE JUDAEO-CHRISTIAN THEORY OF THE GRAIL

Urban T. Holmes, Jr.

In a study published several years ago the present writer proposed that an entirely new viewpoint be used in the interpretation of Chrétien's *Conte del Graal*.[1] If this proposal is to be accepted, the symbols of the Fisher King, the Castle, and the Grail procession, as well as many details throughout Chrétien's poem are representative of the Old Covenant, of the symbols of the Jewish faith. A burning problem of western Europe at the time of the composition of the *Conte del Graal*, between 1275 and 1290, was that of the conversion of the Jews. Anti-Jewish activity seemed to wait only for the accession of the new kings—Philip Augustus in 1180 and Richard the Lion Hearted in 1189—to break out with renewed violence. The older kings, Louis VII and Henry II, had allowed Jewish and Christian institutions to exist side by side in comparative tranquillity. Indeed, as I have pointed out elsewhere, the Count of Guines, an immediate vassal of Philip of Flanders, had a castle in which the chapel was decorated to imitate Solomon's Temple.[2] It will be recalled that this Philip was the patron for whom Chrétien wrote his *Conte del Graal*. If our theory is accepted as correct, then the ultimate purpose of the Grail Quest was not Perceval's personal adoration of the Relics of the Passion: it was something of still greater moment. It was to aid in the transformation of the Relics of the Old Covenant into those of the New. The Holy of Holies of the Jewish Temple contained the cup of Manna, the Rod of Aaron, the silver tablet of the Law, watched over by two Cherubim (who for a mediaeval mind resembled feminine figures). These would be transmuted into the Chalice, the Lance, the cover of the Ciborium, and Angels. The Hall of Solomon's Temple would become Paradise; the wastefully shed blood, which dripped from the Jewish Rod, would be changed to the Sacred Blood shed once by the Christ. This interpretation is suggested in Chapter Nine of the Epistle to the Hebrews.

Naturally, we have searched elsewhere in the writings of the time for confirmation of this solution, for purposefully directed interest in the transmutation of the Jewish symbols into the Christian, and for an active concert in the healing of the Fisher King, whom we identify with Jacob, the High Priest of Israel. While I was discussing this with an outstanding Romance scholar of the

Dominican Order of Nuns, Sister Amelia Klenke, O. P., it became evident to both of us that the Office of Tenebrae (Good Friday) in the Dominican Missal offers some outstanding parallels. Before citing these it would be well to say something of the history of the Dominican Liturgy.[3] Jordan of Saxony's uniform Dominican rite of sometime previous to 1235 was a result of St. Dominic's own study and intention. This was, to be sure, rearranged by the master general Humbert of Romans, 1254-56, and still further amended by the Spanish friar Malvenda at the beginning of the seventeenth century; but the essential parts of the rite remain as a reflection of the older Roman liturgy which came into France in the early eighth century and was still in use there in the twelfth and thirteenth centuries. The Dominicans never adopted 'the later version of the Roman Rite.' There were a few additional elements adopted into the Dominican Rite by the Founder himself and some of these may have come from the Ordinal of the Canons Regular of Prémontré. When St. Dominic founded his Order in Toulouse he adopted the Rule of the Augustinian Canons and some details from the Premonstratensians.[4] The latter Canons were first organized in Champagne in 1119 by St. Norbert, in the Forest of Coucy at Prémontré. If we could establish that the Tenebrae Prayers for the Conversion of the Jews in the Dominican Missal were taken from the Prémontré, we would have an important discovery. Unfortunately, this is a subject which should be investigated by a liturgical scholar; but I have for this the word of Dom Anselm Strittmatter, O. S. B., who is a distinguished liturgist, that a comparison between the Premonstratensian Ordinal and the Dominican Missal might bear fruit.[5]

With respect to the Tenebrae prayers for the Jews, it was the Champenois region which felt most concerned; the Albigensians were a problem that confronted the Dominicans directly in the Toulouse area.

In the Dominican Missal it is the Matins on Good Friday which presents most of the parallels. In the First Nocturn the First Lesson is the Lamentation of Jeremiah, which then closes with "Jerusalem, Jerusalem, convertere ad Dominum Deum tuum." This same refrain is used after the Second Lesson and there follows "Velum templi scissum est, et omnis terra tremuit, etc." The reader may recall that in our Judaeo-Christian theory the name *Perceval* suggests "Perce voile" with reference to the Veil of the Temple.

The Second Nocturn of Good Friday Matins records in the Seventh Lesson that the crime of the Jews exceeds even the blame of Pilate: "Excessit quidem Pilati culpam facinus Judaeorum." Then comes the most striking passage, in the Ninth Lesson:

> You have, O Lord, drawn everything to you, since in execration of the Jewish crime all the Elements have pronounced one and the same sentence ... all creatures have refused to serve the impious ones. You have drawn all to you, O Lord, *for the Veil of the Temple being torn, the Holy of Holies refused entry to the unworthy High Priests, in order that the figure might be transformed into truth, prophecy into fulfilment, Law into the Evangile.* You have brought all to You: *in order that that which was hidden in the Temple of Judaea under obscure symbols, might be celebrated by the devotion of all nations, in a Sacrament visible to all.*[6]

The Mass of the Catechumens ends with prayers for the needs of the Church and closes with words such as these: "Let us pray also for the wicked Jews in order that our Lord God may lift the veil from their hearts and they also may recognize Jesus Christ our Lord." [7]

The passage which we have placed in italics repeats what we consider the heart of the Grail problem: that the obscure symbols of the Holy of Holies may be transformed into the open symbols of the Christian Faith.

The Second Nocturn begins with Psalm 37 which might well have been a lament by the Fisher King.

> ... There is no soundness in my flesh because of Thine anger; neither is there any rest in my bones because of my sin ... I am troubled; I am bowed down greatly; I go mourning all the day long. For my loins are filled with a loathsome disease: and there is no soundness in my flesh. I am feeble and sore broken ... My lovers and my friends stand aloof from my sore; and my kinsmen stand off ... But I, as a deaf man, heard not; and I was as a dumb man that openeth not his mouth.[8]

The Fisher King could not declare his woes to Perceval. But, Perceval, as his kinsman, could break the spell by ceasing to stand aloof, afar off.

The Sarum Missal, which is often cited as being close in many details to the Dominican Rite (they both are based on the older Roman Rite) does not have these elaborations. The conversion of the Jews is given only brief mention at the Tenebrae office.[9] Evidently the Dominicans had a special concern with the conversion of the Jews. Could this have been derived from the Premonstratensians of Champagne in the last quarter of the Twelfth century?

The University of North Carolina

[1] First printed in *Studies in Philology*, XLIV (1947), 453-76, and then republished with a few additions as monograph No. 8 in the University of North Carolina Studies in the Romance Languages and Literatures (Chapel Hill, 1948), 36 pp.

[2] This fact is drawn from the Chronicle of Lambert d'Ardres. I have discussed its import in an article in *Speculum*, XXV (1950), 100-03.

[3] The most accessible authority on this history is W. R. Bonniwell, O. P., *A History of the Dominican Liturgy, 1215-1945* (2nd ed.; New York: Joseph F. Wagner, Inc., 1945). See particularly pp. 118 ff. and 181 ff. The review of this by Dom Anselm Strittmatter in *Speculum*, XXII (1947), 263-72, contains a helpful summary.

[4] That St. Dominic was influenced in the constitutions of his Order by the Prémontré is recorded among others by Louis Moréri, in his *Grand dictionnaire historique*, under "Dominicains." The extent of any influence upon the Dominican Rite is of course not established.

[5] The statement by Dom Anselm is in a letter.

[6] Dominican Missal, p. 486.

[7] *Ibid.*, p. 506.

[8] This is Psalm 38 in the King James English Bible.

[9] *The Sarum Missal, Edited from Three Early Manuscripts*, by J. Wickham Legg (Oxford, 1916), pp. 112 ff.

Jean-Jacques Rousseau and
Anatole France

JEAN-JACQUES ROUSSEAU AND ANATOLE FRANCE
H. R. Huse

When Jean-Jacques Rousseau was developing his paradoxical philosophy, he chose as his starting point the assumption that man is fundamentally good. In America we have generally accepted this flattering dictum. We are not unaware that the Devil, through his wiles, sometimes gets into us, but we are convinced that man was created in the divine image, that he knows right from wrong, and that he is at least wise enough to detect his own interest. This is the rock or sand on which we have erected our institutions and the framework of our beliefs. Nearly all we do or think politically implies faith in man's honesty, justice, and good sense, in free-will and moral responsibility, and in the sacred rights of the sovereign majority.

There was once a reason for this faith. When the old order declined, when the merits that won the privileges of the nobility had disappeared, and when the rising middle classes could contrast their intellectual and moral superiority with the degradation of a corrupt aristocracy, it was not unreasonable to conceive that virtue was a possession of the common man. Moreover, after many centuries of experience in leaving the welfare of the citizen to the tender mercies of oligarchies, priests, kings, and nobles, it was far from unreasonable to suppose that the common man was at least as good a judge of his interests as those who had previously assumed his guardianship. He had fought his kings' private battles long enough, and had sweated enough for the glory of his lords.

Certainly in small, simply organized communities where citizens know each other and where most problems fall within their immediate experience, the voice of the people is often the voice of wisdom if not that of the gods.

But since the days of the frontier and town-meeting the world has changed. It has become smaller, through improved communication, but more complex. Individuals bump into each other more frequently, literally and figuratively, and the important unit is no longer the township or village, but the country as a whole. In this complicated, intricate, and vast society, the serene assumptions of another age no longer apply.

Anatole France attempted to destroy the structure of beliefs and institutions which Rousseau and his followers built on the most gratuitous, arbitrary, and vain of assumptions. France's philosophic system, if it can be called a system, is Rousseauism upside down. It is also, incidentally, a bitter criticism of the most cherished American beliefs.

Imitating Rousseau, France proclaims as loudly as he can the very opposite fundamental assumption, i.e., that man is essentially bad. In so arbitrary a matter, he realizes that no argument or apology is necessary. Whether man is good or bad depends, at best, on a viewpoint, an assumed relationship. We can take as representatives of our kind the heroes, geniuses, and martyrs of the past or present, or, on the other hand, we can look down on those beneath us. Our attitude must vary accordingly. Even a clown doubtless appears godlike to his dog.

In any case, Anatole France chooses deliberately the superior viewpoint, and throughout his works is content to match the Rousseauistic affirmations of man's goodness with equally emphatic denials. He is never weary of pointing out that man is selfish, cowardly, perfidious, gluttonous, and lecherous. Why else would redemption have been neccessary? Do we not all descend from this venerable Eve in whom all our ignoble instincts have their august source? He wonders if Christians have not slandered Satan and the demons. That there may be in some unknown world beings still more vicious than men seems to him possible, although almost inconceivable. In a dozen places he finds occasion to affirm that men are monkeys and ferocious beasts.

The best he can say is that some individuals do have talents and rise above the mass. And yet this talent is precisely what human nature usually pardons least. "In talent there is an insolence that is expiated amid dull hatred and profound calumny." Moreover, excellence of any kind is exclusive to a small number. What is called the genius of a race reaches consciousness only in imperceptible minorities, in a few individuals who think with greater force and precision than the others.

To many, these assertions will appear at best ill-tempered and ungenerous. Our natural inclination is to look up at man, since we are all humble and insignificant and tend to carry into adult life our childish attitudes. To reach a superior viewpoint, we must grow up above the level of most our fellows, which is statistically impossible for the majority. So we tend toward a haughty conception of man. Rousseau's viewpoint was destined to be popular and will remain popular for many a year.

It is one thing, however, for a servant or laborer to believe in his angelic descent and in man's greatness, and another for a philosopher to assume this view. In the latter case we suspect lack of candor. Certainly no superior mind nowadays can share the Rousseauistic notions about the virtuous savage or his sentimental illusions about Nature. We know something of our origin and our atavism. We admit our relationship to our humble ancestors.

But even if the superior viewpoint were not more candid, in France's view, it would be preferable. A curious paradox is involved. An exalted conception of man, strangely, is not only a source of childish illusions, but of cruelties, suffering, and injustice. The political and other beliefs which have caused most blood to flow are precisely those which assume we are rational beings, that we can distinguish clearly between right and wrong, that we are morally responsible, and that our purpose on earth is to regain our angelic stature.

On this point Anatole France is insistent. "Yes," he says, "I have a poor opinion of man, and it is to be hoped that no one should have any other. Otherwise, beware for the human race! Reformers would exact too much. Have you not noticed that the greatest cruelties, the most horrible massacres are inspired by the idea that man is fundamentally good and virtuous? [Those] who led the French Revolution and who drowned France in blood wished precisely to restore primal goodess. They lacked the benevolence and indulgence which a sense of human infirmities gives . . .

"Pride and hatred in the fierce heart of man wish to settle domestic and other difficulties by murder and carnage. The true science of life is a benevolent scorn for men. Let us be humble. Let us not believe we are excellent, for we are not so. In looking at ourselves, let us discover our veritable character which is rough and violent like that of our ancestors, and, since we have the advantage of a longer tradition, let us recognize at least the continuity of our ignorance . . .

"If you are concerned with leading men, you should never forget that they are mischievous monkeys. On that condition alone is a statesman humane and benevolent . . . When you wish to make men good, wise, free, moderate, and generous, you are brought fatally to wishing to kill them all."

The University of North Carolina

Elements of White Magic
In Mediaeval Spanish *Exempla*

ELEMENTS OF WHITE MAGIC IN MEDIAEVAL SPANISH *EXEMPLA*

John E. Keller

The relationship of white magic to Spanish mediaeval *exempla* has never been studied seriously and comprehensively; nevertheless, a close relationship existed, and few were the collections of this form of mediaeval narrative that did not contain colorings and backgrounds in white magic. The present approach to the subject will take the form of a brief introductory study, the aim of which will be that of focusing attention upon the prevalence of white magic in Spanish mediaeval *exempla* repositories and of showing clearly that most of the types or divisions of white magic were represented in them.

A careful examination of the most representative *exempla* collections showed that white magic was present almost throughout the entire period when the *exemplum* flourished, i.e., the 12th through the 15th centuries. Both lay and clerical works drew from the white magic lore of the folk for motifs and subject matter; however, as might be expected, collections of tales compiled by hagiographers employed magic much more extensively than did those repositories whose *exempla* concerned themselves with less exalted matters.

Miracles made up a large percentage of the examples of white magic, but not all miracles can be classified as magic; most miracles, indeed, are based upon faith and the power of prayer, and such miracles did not emerge as a part of folk culture and cannot be considered as true white magic. Sheer faith and its ability to move mountains, heal the sick, raise the dead, and alter the course of nature's laws was an element of the Christian credo of those times: it was not of the folk; it was not white magic; it is not related to the subject of this article. For these reasons all miracles and marvelous happenings in the collections considered, if wrought by faith and faith alone, have been excluded from the study.

The folk—superstitious, credulous, and deeply rooted in an ancient lore of which magic, black and white, was an important part—would not willingly relinquish this age-old heritage. Ecclesiastics, therefore, found it necessary and profitable in their work to borrow deeds once attributed to the pagan gods and popular heroes, grafting these deeds, often with little in the way of modification, upon the new heroes, the saints. If the saints were to supersede the old gods, if the heroes of ancient cultures were to be supplanted, then the hagiographer had to conform to the tastes and beliefs of the people, had to supply, literally upon demand, the magic so deeply embedded in the fibre of the folk.

Magic, we shall consider as a science or art by which the logical, normal forces of nature may be upset, nullified, or made to operate in a fashion not in accord with nature's laws. Unseen, often unknown, almost always incomprehensible forces come into play when magic is practiced, and these forces may be caused to operate for either good or for evil ends. Magic, then, is the art or science of producing preternatural effects through the aid of departed spirits, the occult powers of nature, or mysterious forces beyond the ken of man. Magic is always present to a greater or lesser degree. White magic, magic practiced for ends that are good, magic set in operation by the powers of good, by saints and other holy people, played an important role in Spain's *exempla*. An examination of the varieties of white magic is now in order.

A considerable body of *exempla* was the basis for this study. The collections comprehend chronologically the entire development of the form in Spain from its earliest beginnings, as represented by the *Disciplina clericalis*, through the apogee of literary, popular, recreational, and didactic phases, exemplified by the master works of Don Juan Manuel, Juan Ruiz, and Climente Sánchez. The works whose tales were carefully studied were the following: *El libro de buen amor; El libro de Calila y Dimna; Castigos y documentos del rey don Sancho; El libro del cauallero Zifar; Consolaciones de la vida humana; El corbacho; Disciplina clericalis; El libro de los engaños et los asayamientos de las mugeres; El libro de los estados; El libro de los enxemplos* and *El libro de enxienplos por a.b.c.; El libro de los gatos; El libro de los enxienplos del Conde Lucanor et de Patronio; Milagros de Nuestra Sennora.**

In these works are found more than a thousand *exempla*. Not all contain examples of white magic. The *Disciplina clericalis* might be cited as an example. Some, such as *El libro de los engaños*, contain only examples of black magic. Others are the repositories of numerous illustrations of black and of white magic. Of the last type the best example is *El libro de los enxemplos*.

No effort was made here to catalogue all the examples of white magic present in the collections mentioned above; but a sufficient number of illustrations has been included to strengthen the case for the frequent appearance of white magic in Spanish works of the *exemplum* genre.

The religious *exempla* collections, as has been noted, contain the greatest number of examples of white magic. Of these, the most numerous samples appear in *El libro de los enxemplos, Consolaciones de la vida humana, Castigos y documentos del rey don Sancho,* and *Milagros de Nuestra Sennora*.

The divisions employed here for convenience in the treatment of the types of white magic in mediaeval Spanish *exempla* collections are those used by Stith Thompson,[1] namely, A. Mythological Motifs, in which magic animals are included; D. Magic, under which are found magic transformation, magic control of the elements, magic invulnerability, destructive magic powers, magic automata, and miscellaneous magic manifestations; F. Marvels, wherein are listed magic powers of perception, extraordinary plants that undergo miraculous growth, and magic multiplication; Q. Rewards and Punishments, the section that lists miraculous rewards and punishments; V. Religion, the section devoted to miraculous images, the saints, angels, the Virgin Mary, et cetera.

Magic animals

Motifs employing magic animals were quite common in the Spanish works studied: a dragon guarded the food of a holy hermit, frightened robbers so violently as to bring about their repentance;[2] bees left honey on the lips of a child destined to become a great man, and ants brought grains of wheat to another child whose future was bright;[3] a hyena guided a lost hermit out of the wilderness;[4] wild leopards accompanied the Holy Family through the desert on their flight into Egypt;[5] birds showed a monk where to dig for a hidden treasure.[6]

Magic transformation

Magic transformations were not uncommon. Sometimes the transformation was made from a human being to an animal, as when a holy hermit changed a girl into a mouse;[7] in a very graphic illustration of white magic transformation a saint caused maggots in a holy nun's sore to become precious gems;[8] water changed into wine in another *exemplum*.[9]

Magic control of the elements

In Spanish *exempla* saints and holy people control the elements with apparent ease: magic winds, raised at the command of saints, are present in at least three of the collections;[10] with a magic iron rod another saint made bodies of water open and close.[11]

Magic charms, talismans, and words

Among some of the most interesting and authentic examples of folk magic found in the *exempla* collections are those in which the saint employs a charm, talisman or magic word to bring about some miracle. Stories of this kind vividly illustrate the powerful underlying influence of the folk culture of Spain. A woman, beset nightly by the devil, is able to ward off his unwanted attentions by sleeping with the hose of a saint;[12] an evil spirit is adjured to depart by naming the Deity;[13] the sign of the cross is all that is required to banish the devil, in one case, [14] and wild beasts, in another; [15] holy water washes away marks left upon a man's face by the Fiend;[16] witchcraft involving the spirit of a dead child that attempts to lead its mother into peril is overcome by burning a lock of the dead infant's hair.[17]

In these examples the magic of the folk has been transplanted bodily into the soil Christian white magic. One is led to believe that the clergyman[18] who used these instances of magic in a book designed to provide preachers with sermon topics was of the folk, and that he knew the folk remedies for averting supernatural perils so well that he allowed these old remedies to creep into his text with the more legitimate Christian miracles.

Magic powers of perception; magic senses

The magic of the saints gave them the power to foresee dangers, to be aware of events long before they happened, to see through solid matter, and to predict the future. All of these powers are well represented in the collections studied: a saint was able to warn a boy of a serpent that had hidden in a basket left by the child in a distant spot;[19] a blind holy man was aware that a man was poisoning his drink;[20] when pilgrims hid their clothing in a wood and begged a saint to clothe them, he was able to see the hidden garments and to send the false beggars away.[21]

Magic invulnerability

The magic invulnerability afforded certain saints was truly remarkable: fire consumed a house in which a saint was residing, burned the clothing from his back, but left the holy flesh unharmed;[22] another saint handled the most venomous serpents with no danger to his life;[23] more marvelous still was a saint who drank poison and suffered no ill effects.[24]

Saints were able to impart magic invulnerability to others whom they desired to protect: a saint sustained a man on the gallows for several days until his innocence had been established;[25] a young prince of holy inclinations was saved from murder at the hands of his uncle by a group of infant angels who slew his assailants.[26]

Celestial visitors; angels, the Virgin, et cetera

The appearance of celestial visitors in Spanish *exempla* collections merits study. Likewise, some study of the visitations of the Holy Virgin would seem to deserve a separate investigation. The Virgin appeared in so many of these Spanish *exempla* that no study, however brief, would be complete without at least some minor treatment of her place in the literature.

Berceo's *Milagros de Nuestra Sennora* is a collection of twenty-five miracles of the Virgin. *El libro de los enxemplos* in both its manuscripts devotes a great deal of space and a great many *exempla* to miracles and marvelous cures and protection afforded by the Mother of God. A few examples will have to suffice here to illustrate the folklore of the Virgin in the Spanish *exempla* repositories: the Virgin supported a man on the gallows because he was one of her devotees;[27] she resuscitated a drowned man;[28] she restored the hand to a saint after he had cut if off in an attempt to suppress lust;[29] she destroyed a great Moorish army at the gates of Constantinople;[30] she rescued a man from a watery grave after a shipwreck.[31]

Destructive magic power; magic punishment

Not always did the saints and holy hermits and pious nuns turn white magic into channels of kindness: at times it was necessary for them to destroy their enemies and the foes of their faith. A few examples will serve to explain the statement. A holy woman, a near-saint, was accused by her husband of infidelity. Innocent, she appealed for some sign to prove that she was guiltless. Her husband immediately became a leper.[32] A knight ravished a holy nun and then took flight on his horse. Miraculously, the nun appeared in front of him on the animal, grasped the reins and held them with such supernatural strength that those pursuing the knight were able to overtake and apprehend him.[33] One saint ruined a fine sword belonging to a man about to execute a good woman; the sword was hopelessly dulled.³⁴ A lewd girl, about to bear an illegitimate child, accused a holy bishop of fathering the unborn infant. She was kept in a state of miraculously and phenomenally prolonged labor until she confessed and absolved the bishop of all blame.³⁵

Magic automata

Inanimate objects such as statues, images, the cross, and even things like trees and springs may be imbued with magic powers: a magic statue revealed a treasure;³⁶ an image of the Saviour descended from the cross to punish a nun about to desert the convent and flee with a lover;³⁷ His image bled when injured by a Jew;³⁸ a statue of the Virgin grasped the hem of an artist's garment when the devil pushed him from a lofty scaffolding.³⁹ The Virgin once wove a magic garment for an exceptionally pious priest. When an evil priest put the garment on, it strangled him to death.⁴⁰

Miraculous growth and multiplication

Miraculous growth and multiplication was a favorite subject of the compilers of *exempla* and probably of the folk. Such miracles were doubtless suggested, in part at least, by Scripture; but it is possible, and even very likely, that marvels of this kind had formed a part of the lore of the people, for all peoples seem to produce such tales.

Vegetables and fruits matured in an unbelievably short time—indeed, they developed even as people watched them;⁴¹ certain monks were so pious that their supply of flour was never low, even when they gave quantities away daily to the poor;⁴² one amusing tale tells of a saint who cast dice with a man for the latter's soul, and caused the dice to split so as to make a higher score for himself.⁴³

Closely related to this sort of magic multiplication is the miracle of the inexplicable replacement of objects removed by saints or of false relics made authentic for holy people. St. Nicholas, in order to feed the poor, was obliged to steal certain supplies of bread. Before the theft could be discovered, the bread was miraculously restored.⁴⁴ In another case, a man bought a finger which he believed to be a relic of a saint. The finger was not authentic; nevertheless, because of his piety, he soon received the true finger, which was missing thereafter from the corpse of the saint.⁴⁵

White magic, then, was well represented in mediaeval Spanish exempla collections of both lay and clerical authorship. Indeed, during the course of this investigation, motifs founded upon magic, white and black, were found to be numerous enough to merit separate studies. It is seen that the principal divisions or types of white magic are represented in the Spanish collections, and there are indications pointing to the probable use of the various types or divisions of black magic.

The Spanish *exemplum* genre gathered and perpetuated numerous magic motifs which otherwise might well have been lost, since they do not appear in other literatures. Many of these motifs, it is true, were not original to Spanish writing; on the other hand, a large number of them may have appeared first in Spain. The difficulties involved in determining the origins of tales are well known. In many cases there is no certainty as to whether a motif was common lore, or not. Conclusions of this nature are so difficult to reach that it is often necessary to depend upon a feeling for motifs of Spanish background, and obviously such feelings are not reliable.

The University of Tennessee

* The titles of these collections are abbreviated as follows:

Barlaam, ed. Lauchert, Friedrich. "La estoria del rey Anemur e de Iosaphat e de Barlaam," *Romanische Forschüngen*, VII (1893), 33-402;

Buen Amor, ed. Cejador y Frauca, Julio. *Juan Ruiz Arcipreste de Hita, Libro de buen amor* (Vol. 1) (Madrid: Espasa-Calpe, 1937: Vol. II) 1941);

Calila, ed. Alemany, J. *La antigua versión del Calila y Dimna cotejada con el original árabe de la misma* (Madrid: Librería de los sucesores de Hernando, 1915);

Castigos, ed. Gayangos, Pascual de. *Castigos e documentos del rey don Sancho*, B.A.E. Vol. 51 (Madrid: Rivadeneyra, 1912, 79-228);

Zifar, ed. Wagner, C. P. *El libro del cauallero Zifar* (Ann Arbor: University of Michigan, 1929);

Consolaciones, ed. Gayangos, Pascual de. *Libro de las consolaciones de la vida humana*, B.A.E. Vol. 51 (Madrid: Rivadeneyra, 1912, 561-602);

Corbacho, ed. Simpson, Lesley Byrd. *Alfonso Martínez de Toledo. El arcipreste de Talavera o sea El corbacho* (Berkley: University of California Press, 1939).

Disciplina, ed. Hilka, Alfons and Werner Soderhjelm. *Die Disciplina Clericalis des Petrus Alfonsi* (Heidelburg: Carl Winter's Universitatbuchhandlung, 1911);

Engaños, ed. Comparetti, Domenico. *Researches Respecting the Book of Sindibad* (London: Elliot Stock, 1882);

Estados, ed. Gayangos, Pascual de. *El libro de los estados*, B.A.E. Vol. 51 (Madrid: Rivadeneyra, 1912) pp. 278-363;

Enxemplos (G), for Libro de los enxemplos, ed. Gayangos, Pascual de. *El libro* de los enxempla, B.A.F. Vol. 51 (Madrid, Rivadeneyra, 1912) pp. 443-542;

Enxemplos (M), for Libro de los enxienplos por a.b.c. ed. Morel-Fatio, F. "El libro de los enxienplos por a.b.c. de Climente Sanchez de Valderas," Romania, VII (1878), 481-526;

Gatos, ed. Gayangos, Pascual de. El libro de los gatos, B.A.E. Vol 51, (Madrid: Rivadeneyra, 1912) pp. 543-60;

Lucanor, ed. Knust, Herman and Adolf Birch-Hirschfeld. Juan Manuel el libro de los enxiemplos del Conde Lucanor et de Patronio (Leipzig: Dr. Seele and Co., 1900);

Milagros, ed. Janer, Florencio. Milagros de Nuestra Sennora, B.A.E. Vol. 57 (Madrid: Librería y Casa Editorial Hernando, 1925), pp. 103-131.

[1] Stith Thompson, Motif-Index of Folk Literature (Indiana University Studies; Bloomington, Indiana, 1932-36).

[2] Enxemplos (G), no. 377; Enxemplos (M), no. 3.

[3] Ibid., no. 109.

[4] Ibid., no. 50

[5] Castigos, p. 145.

[6] Calila, p. 453.

[7] Ibid., p. 289.

[8] Enxemplos (G), no. 277.

[9] Consolaciones, p. 369.

[10] Castigos, p. 108; Enxemplos (M), no. 33; Enxemplos (G), no. 206.

[11] Castigos, pp. 104, 122, 226.

[12] Enxemplos (G), no. 45.

[13] Ibid., no. 86.

[14] Ibid., no. 21; Buen Amor, I, 196.

[15] Barlaam, p. 390.

[16] Enxemplos (G), no. 125.

[17] Ibid., no. 378.

[18] The clergyman was Climente Sánchez, the Archdeacon of Valderas, who included several of these motifs in his El libro de los enxemplos, suggesting them as topics for sermons.

[19] Enxemplos (G), no. 337.

[20] Ibid., no. 170.

[21] Ibid., no. 322.

[22] Ibid., no. 333; Consolaciones, p. 567; Milagros, no. 13.

[23] Estados, p. 313.

[24] Loc. cit.

[25] Enxemplos (G), nos. 222, 223; Enxemplos (M), no. 33

[26] Zifar, p. 271.

[27] Enxemplos (G), no. 201; Enxemplos (M), no. 48; Milagros, no. 6.

[28] Enxemplos (G), no. 198.

[29] Ibid., nos. 204, 335.

[30] Ibid., no. 206.

[31] Ibid., no. 213.

[32] Lucanor, no. 44.

[33] Castigos, p. 130.

[34] Enxemplos (M), no. 14.

[35] Enxemplos (G), nos. 18, 216.

[36] *Ibid.*, no. 172.
[37] *Castigos*, p. 130.
[38] *Enxemplos* (G), nos. 19, 20.
[39] *Ibid.*, no. 194.
[40] *Milagros*, no. 1.
[41] *Zifar*, p. 226.
[42] *Enxemplos* (G), nos. 75, 76.
[43] *Ibid.*, no. 183.
[44] *Castigos*, p. 99.
[45] *Enxemplos* (G), no. 132.

Did Calderon Have a Sense of Humor?

DID CALDERON HAVE A SENSE OF HUMOR?

Sturgis E. Leavitt

Dramatic technique of the Golden Age in Spain was more or less standardized by Lope de Vega, whose success with the public was no encouragement for others to deviate from his procedures. And yet, within established broad lines, Lope's numerous rivals developed their own particular talents, some of them very successfully. Guillén de Castro, for example, is notable for his handling of the *romances,* Tirso de Molina for his women characters, and Alarcón for his everyday touches and moral purpose. There are many others who found ways to be original without crossing the loosely set barriers that hedged them in.

One of the elements of the *comedia* most successfully developed by Lope after he had reached the height of his career was the *gracioso*. This character at times has an important part in the action, at other times not. He has something funny to say on most occasions, and his remarks must have contributed no little to Lope's popularity with the crowd. This good lead was followed to some extent by Guillén de Castro, and to a considerable degree by Tirso and Alarcón. In the case of the last two playwrights the *graciosos* are as different from Lope's as two worlds, but they all have one trait in common. They are funny.

Faced with the necessity of amusing a rough and ready audience, the playwright found his *gracioso* a definite asset—provided the character had a sense of humor. But a supposedly funny character that did not live up to expectations could hardly have been anything but a liability to both playwright and actors. At first glance this dreadful handicap seems to have been wished upon Calderón. He appears to have had a comic character thrust into his lap, and apparently he was hard put to make this personage even moderately funny.

If we examine the *graciosos* in the serious plays of Calderón, we find the most ghastly attempts at humor in the whole history of the Spanish stage. In some of these plays, indeed, this particular character could well have been dispensed with, had it not been that Calderón evidently thought that something of this kind was expected. *El príncipe constante* is one of these plays, and here the funniest thing the *gracioso*, Brito, can do is to get trampled on by the Moors, and then in a sudden and unlikely fit of bravery drive the Moors away with a sentence in Portuguese. In *La vida es sueño* the *gracioso* succeeds in getting killed. There is no fun intended in this, the only case perhaps of a *gracioso's* death on the Spanish stage; it merely illustrates one of the philosophical points the author wishes to drive home. But before he passes from the scene, this man Clarín springs mediocre joke after mediocre joke based principally upon his own cowardice. The one good bit of humor that he contributes to the gaiety of nations seems to be a wild hit in the dark, the sort of thing that might happen by accident once in a thousand years. When Clarín's "master" Rosaura, in giving up her sword, declares she can surrender it only to a person of high degree, Clarín says to one of the common soldiers:

> La mía es tal, que puede darse
> Al más ruin: tomadla vos.

In the less serious plays, such as those of the *capa y espada* type, Calderón's humor can be quite as uninspired as in his serious efforts. A striking example of an all-out attempt to be funny is to be found in *Casa con dos puertas mala es de guardar*. Here the author has the *gracioso* put on a little play, something in the style of Serafina in Tirso's *Vergonzoso en palacio*. Calabazas thanks his master for giving him a ready-made suit, which will obviate the necessity of having one made by a tailor. The *gracioso* takes two parts, that of the customer and that of the tailor, and for some seventy mortal lines enacts the process of ordering the suit and trying it on. The scene is dull in the extreme, and Calabazas' master evidently thinks so, too, for his comment after it is over is "Qué locuras!" Incidentally, it frequently happens that Calderón thus depreciates his own humor.

Examples of this kind could be multiplied, with an assembly of cheap *graciosos*, wooden creatures who are ignorant, unintelligent, and unimaginative. All would be well, and the question could easily be decided in the negative, were it not for a case like *La dama duende*. In this play Calderón presents a *gracioso* who, if not the best in the whole field of *siglo de oro* plays, is without question well toward the front. Cosme, the *gracioso* under discussion, is educated to the point of having seen a number of plays—he is reminded of them by present circumstances; and he is quick witted—when asked to explain why he said he couldn't read (he had made a slip and revealed that he could), he answers that he can read books, but not hand-writing. He can curse eloquently—"Doscientos mil demonios De su furia infernal den testimonios . . ." He carries on a debate with himself about the advisability of going out to pray in a monastery—get a drink in a saloon. He is afraid of ghosts, and there are many humorous scenes in which this trait counts heavily. He has a private philosophy of his own —when his master says the ghost cannot be a demon but must be a woman, Cosme's answer is "Todo es uno." This character has humorous lines, is placed in many humorous situations, and is naturally a funny man in his own right. Cosme is really the best developed character in the play, and there is grave danger of his stealing the show. If one were to judge from *La dama duende* alone, one would say that Calderón was the greatest humorist in Golden Age drama.

The University of North Carolina

A Comic Enchantment in the *Perceforest*

A COMIC ENCHANTMENT IN THE *PERCEFOREST*
Robert G. Lewis

Magic was an important feature of the literature of the Middle Ages. It added wonder to the early works by the mystery of its spells and the awful, inexorable punishment for the breaking of its taboos. When it was used sparingly it did not detract from the individual prowess of the heroes. As later writers of courtly romances multiplied the adventures of an increasing number of Arthurian heroes they leaned more heavily on magic. By the fourteenth century these adventures had become commonplace, and spells and enchantments were employed promiscuously to reinforce the effect of traditional episodes rehandled. In the *Perceforest* materials from several main streams of narrative are combined without achieving new vigor. Magic undergoes a similar change, and in this work it is even employed for comic effect.

In the incident under consideration, King Alexander and several of his knights are fighting in unequal combat against several knights of the lineage of Darnant the Enchanter. When these evil knights see themselves being worsted, they decide to escape.

> Entre lesquels avoit un chevalier nepveu de darnant qui dist a ses compaignons—beausseigneurs nous ne pouvons meshui que perdre et me semble bon de retourner puis que force nest pas pour nous et leur joueray dun jeu. Lors fist un enchantement quil fu advis au roy et aux autres quilz estoient montez chacun sur ung aisne.
> Quant le roy se vey en ce point comme esbahy et la veue trouble il dist a ses compaignons—Jay change mon mestier et suis devenu monnier/ certes dist le tor vous netes dont pas preudomme/ et si je ne le suis dist le roy si ne le semble je pas. Par ma foy dist le tor a grant peine me changeray puis que je suis carbonnier car mon asne est chargie de charbon. Gadiffer lui respondy dieu le vous doinst tost vendre pour raler a lautre. Beausire dist le tor qui etes vous qui vous gabez de ma marchandise. Et Gadiffer dist il me semble que cest beurre que je maine portez la dist le tor en la cuisine si mangerez la grasse soupe. Ainsi se retrouvoient les nobles barons par lenchantement qui avoit este fait sur eulx. Mais le debat etoit beaucoup plus grant entre porus et estonne car porus disoit a estonne. Il mest advis beausire que vous menez pain vendez nous ent. Et estonne qui avoit la teste esmeute lui respondoit/ Mais vous qui menez a boire vous nirez plus avant saurons beu, et prent son asne par le frain. Cassel etoit delez porus qui disoit beausire nous beuverons sil vous plaist, car nouveau marchant doit paier son entree. Puisque ainse est dist porus je lottroy et en tastez. Adont Cassel qui etoit tout desvoie lui cuida baillier ung pot mais il lui presenta son heaulme. Et porus cuide venir a son tonnel et prendre la broche mais lenchantement failly qui ne pouvoit plus durer. Lors

> revindrent tous en leur bon sens et voient que porus tenoit la queue de son cheval et son heaulme dessoubz. Adont ils se prendrent tous a rire sinon porrus qui se print a courrouchier.[1]

The magician who casts this spell is a member of a numerous family of evil enchanters. Their knowledge comes ultimately from Cassandra, who, according to the story, escaped from Troy and came to Britain where she taught magic to the inhabitants. She was later punished for this because her pupils used her arts for wicked ends. In succeeding generations, the malevolent distortion of Cassandra's lore was concentrated mainly in the family of Darnant. The most common manifestations of their skill consist of disguising themselves or others by illusion, creating magic rivers and hiding castles by surrounding walls of thick air. However, these same powers are also found with equal frequency among the benevolent magicians, most of whom are women.

There are several unusual features of the enchantment itself. First, it is gradual in its effect. The horses are seemingly transformed, and by degrees the knights become aware of the change in themselves and call their companions' attention to it. Second, the spell is of short duration ("mais lenchantement failly qui ne pouvoit plus durer"). Third, there is a constant insistence upon the fact that the change is illusory. The king is "comme esbahy" and his sight is "trouble"; Estonne has "la teste esmeute"; Cassel is "tout desvoie"; finally they return to "leur bon sens." Fourth, the intention ("et leur joueray dun jeu") and the outcome are not disastrous.

Transformation occurs frequently in literary magic, although, with the exception of lycanthropy, it is relatively rare in primitive practices.[2] Most of the cases in the literature of antiquity do not offer real parallels. Circe and Medea did not cast their spells for comic purposes. In the *Golden Ass* we find comic transformations; but in the chief one the hero is actually turned into an ass, even though he retains a tender skin and human understanding.[3] The earlier episode in which Lucius is tried for murder in honor of the God of Laughter depends as much on his intoxicated state on leaving the banquet as it does upon witchcraft.

We find a limited parallel to the *Perceforest* enchantment in Saint Augustine, who discounts classic tales of transformation, but says that such things are still believed. He gives as an example the report that Italian milkmaids turn travelers into oxen and put them to work. He also recounts the tale of one Praestantius, who fell into a deep stupor for days and, waking, said that he had dreamed he was a horse carrying corn to soldiers—which, upon inquiry, was found to have been so.[4]

There are also partial parallels among the Irish, whose druids, satirists, and saints practiced magic and were able to cause "sight-shifting," a temporary illusion. Plummer cites examples of laymen appearing to be clerics, of a man appearing to be a woman carrying a child, and of a man or a horse taken for a log.[5] There is also the famous incident of Saint Patrick's *Lorica* (or Breastplate), which had such power that, when its verses were chanted by Patrick, he and his followers appeared to their enemies in the likeness of a herd of deer and in this guise escaped dangerous pursuit.[6]

The comic *intention* that is a striking feature of enchantment in the *Perceforest* differentiates it from the closest parallels cited above. The passage with which we are concerned is an example of gay, sophisticated magic rather than a presentation of popular belief. Its purpose is to amuse the reader and at the same time to furnish a means of terminating an episode, while leaving both the magicians and the knights in a position to participate in further adventures.

Too often in the *Perceforest* magic is used as a substitute for careful planning and motivation of action. It creates artificial difficulties for the protagonists so that the real prowess of the good knights is diminished. Magic is employed on the slightest provocation; and, since both good and evil characters practice it, magical skill rather than human feats becomes the center of attention. Alexander the Great is made a buffoon, and magic becomes facile, even a joke.

Duke University

[1] Bibliothèque de l'Arsenal MS. 3483, f. 113.

[2] Cf. Sir James Frazer, *The Golden Bough* (London: Macmillan and Co., 1917), and Hutton Webster, *Magic: A Sociological Study* (Stanford, California: Stanford University Press, 1948), pp. 160, 182.

[3] While the transformation of Lucius is gradual, the spell has to be broken by a specific counter-spell, the eating of a bunch of roses. (Cf. Apuleius, *The Golden Ass* [The Loeb Classical Library ed.; London and New York, 1935], p. 561.)

[4] Cf. H. C. Lea, *Materials toward a History of Witchcraft*, arranged and edited by A. C. Howland (Philadelphia: University of Pennsylvania Press, 1939), I, 124.

[5] Carolus Plummer, *Vitae sanctorum hiberniae* (Oxonii: E typographeo Clarendoniano, MCMX), I, clxix.

[6] For a translation of the *Lorica* of Saint Patrick, see Kuno Meyer, *Selections from Ancient Irish Poetry* (2d.ed.; London: Constable and Co., Ltd., 1913), pp. 25-27.

Non-Classical French Criticism in the
Mid-Seventeenth Century

NON-CLASSICAL FRENCH CRITICISM IN THE MID-SEVENTEENTH CENTURY: CHARLES SOREL AND HIS *BIBLIOTHEQUE FRANCOISE*

John Coriden Lyons

Even in this day, when research in the French 17th century has developed enough evidence to make the statement manifestly inaccurate, it is not unusual to see scholars and critics refer to that era as "the age of classicism." When a specialist in the period indulges in this trite and easy simplification, he does so with a myriad of mental reservations. He knows quite well that, even at the height of the movement, there were a great many literary people who did not accept the validity of the critical standards laid down by Boileau. It is even debatable whether the classical thesis represented the opinion of a majority of those who were putting quill to paper at that time. The prestige which the "sage of Auteuil" acquired with later generations has blinded us, I think, to the energetic opposition which his ideas encountered in his own day.

In the decades preceding 1660, the period commonly referred to in the manuals in black-faced type as the "era of pre-classicism," the above statements are many times more true. At the time that Jean Chapelain and some of his contemporaries were elaborating the dogma of classicism and laying the foundations for Boileau's success, there was little to indicate to the literary public of that day that these standards would eventually prevail and would come to be regarded by future generations as the characteristic earmark of 17th century French literature. While they could hardly fail to be aware of that body of critical dogma which we today call "classicism," it is safe to say that more than a few critics in the period before 1660 looked on these tenets as *only one* kind of standard; they did not propose to reject or condemn outright works which had followed quite different formulas of literary composition.

To illustrate the foregoing statements, I have selected a too-little-known work by one of the most picturesque figures of the first half of the French 17the century, the *Bibliothèque françoise* of Charles Sorel. While this work appeared only in 1664, at a time when Boileau was already penning his first *Satires*, we must remember that the author was at that time an old man in his sixties. To grasp the full significance of the *Bibliothèque françoise* and place the work in its proper setting, we must look on the ideas and viewpoints expressed by Sorel as belonging to a day when he was in his prime, and to the heyday of his literary activity,— namely, the 1620's, 30's and 40's. Everything about the work justifies taking this position. Both the volume of items mentioned and the relative emphasis he places in examining them show that Sorel was living very much in the past when he published his *Bibliothèque françoise* in 1664.

The name of Charles Sorel (1599-1674) is not one of those best known to students of 17th century French literature. The standard reference (E. Roy: *La vie et les oeuvres de Charles Sorel* [Paris: Hachette, 1891]) cannot be considered very satisfactory by modern standards of scholarship. Two of Sorel's contemporaries have left piquant if sketchy portraits of our author; the first of these is a friendly appreciation by the celebrated doctor-letter writer, Gui Patin, in a letter dated Nov. 25, 1653, and the second is a caricature by Antone Furetière in the *Roman bourgeois*. To establish a picture of Sorel as a person, I quote selected fragments from these two sources:

> *Patin*: "C'est un petit homme grasset avec un grand nez aigu qui regarde de près, âgé de 54 ans, qui paraît fort mélancolique et ne l'est point . . . Il a fait beaucoup de livres français . . . il a encore plus de vingt volumes à faire, et voudrait bien que tout cela fût fait avant que de mourir, mais ne peut venir à bout des imprimeurs. Il est fort délicat et je l'ai souvent vu malade: néanmoins il vit commodément parce qu'il est fort sobre . . . Je ne suis point sçavant comme lui."[2]
>
> *Furetière*: "Son nez, qu'on pouvait à bon droit appeler Son Eminence, et qui était toujours vêtu de rouge, avait été fait en apparence pour un colosse: néanmoins il avait été donné à un homme de taille assez courte. Ce n'est pas que la nature ait rien fait perdre à ce petit homme, car ce qu'elle lui avait ôté en hauteur, elle le lui avait rendu en grosseur, de sorte qu'on lui trouvait assez de chair, mais fort mal pétrie. Sa chevelure était la plus désagréable du monde . . . .; aussi ne se peignait-il jamais qu'avec les doigts . . . Sa peau était grenue comme celle des maroquins, et sa couleur brune était réchauffée par de rouges bourgeons qui la perçaient en assez bon nombre. En général, il avait une mine de satyre . . . Ses yeux gros et bouffis avient quelque chose de plus que d'être à fleur de tête. Jamais il n'y eut un homme plus médisant ni plus envieux."[3]

Sorel is best known to students of 17th century French literature as the author of three "realistic" novels: *L'histoire comique de Francion* (1622), *Le berger extravagant* (1627), and *Polyandre* (1648). We know from his own statement that these three works were currently attributed to him in his own lifetime, and posterity has confirmed this attribution by crediting him with them ever since. Yet in the last chapter of the *Bibliothèque françoise* he devotes some twenty pages[4] to a vigorous denial of the authorship of these three works and a number of other well-known ones which have been attributed to him also. We have noted above the statement of Gui Patin: "Il a fait beaucoup de livres français . . . il a encore plus de vingt volumes à faire." In the latter part of the chapter just mentioned,[5] Sorel admits the authorship of many such volumes; most of them are titles in the historical, moral and philosophic fields.

Why, then, does Sorel deny authorship of the three novels (which had appeared respectively forty-two, thirty-seven, and sixteen years before the *Bibliothèque françoise*) if he had actually written them? . . . The care with which he examines them and the amount of time he devotes to their consideration, as compared with what he devotes to other similar works of the same period, lead one to suspect that he had more than a passing interest in and affection for these three novels. We sense in the tone of his statements, in the readiness with which he points out that the three works have much to commend them, a certain subjective concern which he does not show for other works of the same nature. He says further that the authors of these works need certainly feel no shame for having written them. I feel that posterity is correct in attributing these novels to Sorel, and offer a simple theory as to why he felt in 1664 that he could not afford to admit authorship.

In 1664 Sorel was an old man about to transmit his reputation to the judgment of posterity. Considering the reputation he seems to have enjoyed at that time, and in view of the nature of the works for which he willingly admitted authorship in the *Bibliothèque françoise*, there seems to me to be little doubt that he wanted his name to go down to future generations as that of a serious and erudite scholar. The trivialities, irreverences, and occasional indecencies which mark the pages of the three novels may easily have seemed to him to be out of keeping with the kind of reputation he wanted to leave behind him. Furthermore, the accepted tone of what was permissible had changed by 1664. Liberties and even licences which might have been forgiven a young man writing in the 1620's could be damaging to the reputation of an aged scholar if admitted in the 1660's. In short, I believe that Sorel was secretly proud of the success which had been attained by his "folies de jeunesse," but felt that the serious reputation he wanted to bequeath to posterity could not afford the possible stigma of having the irreverent works of his youth publicly acknowledged by him.

We now turn to the main point of this article: an examination of Sorel's criteria of literary evaluation. In this field Sorel continues in modified form the sixteenth century tradition which presented with little indication of preference all the works which had been written in a given field. But Sorel *does* inject the notion that *all* works are not to be accepted indiscriminately. Commenting on the *Bibliothèques françoises* of La Croix du Maine and Antoine du Verdier, our author observes that one should not follow *ce vieux dessein* too closely. Many books have been written that it would be better to forget. By selecting a limited number of the works in a given field, it is easier to form a considered judgment.[6]

However, even though he feels that many inferior works might be left unmentioned, Sorel does not propose to inflict on his reader any fixed opinion about the relative value of those he does present. He will not be presumptuous or overbearing enough to dictate to his readers how they should feel about any particular work; he will not set himself up as a court of final authority. The opinions he presents are those he believes to be generally accepted by the literary people of his time; in presenting them, Sorel emphasizes that he does not intend to deprive the reader of the right to form his own private opinion. It is his desire to interest his readers in all sorts of literary works. He does not want to discourage his public by insisting on any one absolute dogma. *Supposé qu'il ait nommé autant de mauvais livres que de bons, c'est afin que les personnes d'esprit tirent leur profit de toutes choses.*[7] We might note that at this very moment Boileau was setting forth ideas which were far less tolerant.

Sorel's tolerance as a critic appears with great clarity in the attitude he took with regard to the standards of linguistic usage which were under discussion at the time.[8] The points he makes show his opposition to any form of absolutism. He criticizes the positive positions which had been taken earlier by Henri Estienne in his *Dialogues du nouveau langage françois italianisé*. We know that this was a controversial work and that Estienne was a propagandist for French nationalism subsidized by Henri III. Sorel sensed this state of affairs and condemned Estienne for having been opinionated and obviously partial. He dismisses Malherbe rather brusquely: *M. de Malherbe en avoit donné quequesrègles ... mais cela estoit gardé secrettement dans une espèce de caballe où le vulgaire avoit peine à pénétrer.*

Judging the controvery over linguistic usage between Vaugelas and La Mothe Le Vayer, Sorel's sympathies were with the latter author. We should recall that La Mothe Le Vayer, academician, socialite and man of the world was regarded by contemporaries as the inveterate enemy of all postive attitudes toward anything, including language. Speaking of his *Considérations sur l'éloquence françoise de ce temps*, Sorel comments: *Il a cela de particulier qu'il s'oppose hardiment au retranchement de mots que veulent faire quelque grammairiens.*[9] While Sorel recognizes the values of the work of Vaugelas, he objects very strongly to the tone of finality assumed by the author of the *Remarques*.

In his third chapter, *Des livres de philosophie*, the abundant citations reflect the extensive and intensive interest of the intellectual public of the French 17th century in all aspects of the natural sciences. The citations run from Plato, Aristotle, and Plutarch among the ancients to Bacon, Descartes, and Pascal among the moderns. While there are no specific statements in this chapter to indicate Sorel's opinion about the principles of classicism, the eclectic nature of his references and the heterogeneous mass of works which he mentions are at the opposite pole from the fixed standards of literary, aristic, and intellectual classicism.

As he considers books which treat of moral codes,[10] Sorel tells us that it makes little difference where the doctrine comes from, providing that it contributes something useful. One should give consideration to all sorts of diverse ideas, regardless of their source. These statements support an idea already suggested: that Sorel and his generation were eclectics rather than classicists, that they did not accept any one system or set of standards to the exclusion of all others. I believe that Sorel accepted classicism as *one* valid set of critical criteria but would not reject works which did not conform to this standard as being, of necessity, artistically inferior or reprehensible.

The above contention is substantiated by his general appreciation of the novels of the day—a *genre* of which Boileau was to make such high mockery a short while later. He feels that each of these novels has its own special merit and that some even possess several sorts of beauty.[11] One might apply to the novels Sorel's statement about the epic poems of the day: *Les poèmes héroïques ont esté aussi critiquez diversement.*[12]

It is with the field of the drama that we usually associate most closely the crystallization of the doctrine of classicism in 17th century France. Sorel includes his discussion of this subject in a general chapter on poetry. He hardly mentions the unities. As he surveys the field from 1618 to 1664, he lists indiscriminately pastorals, "irregular" tragi-comedies, comedies, and tragedies. He feels that Corneille may have sinned against the laws of the stage and of poetry; but he had not failed to please and be applauded, *et c'est le vray secret de l'art*.[13] Sorel's mention of the labors of the Abbé d'Aubignac and La Mesnardière is so casual as to make one feel that he attached no particular importance to the doctrine of dramatic classicism.

In summary, if we are to take Sorel's *Bibliothèque françoise* as being at all representative of the opinion of the decades in which he had led his active life, the doctrine of classicism did not dominate the thought of the literary public in France before 1660. In this work, Sorel was leaving a literary legacy to posterity. In view of his reputation and all we know about him, it is safe to conjecture that he would not have expressed himself as he did if he had felt that his views were not shared by a considerable body of his contemporaries. Even if we did not have an abundance of other evidence to support our argument, it would be unlikely that the cautious Sorel would ever let himself be placed in the position of a lone wolf howling in the wilderness. Therefore, it seems to me that the ideas expressed by Charles Sorel in the *Bibliothèque françoise* offer the best sort of proof that the tenets of classicism were not accepted by the French literary public of the first half of the 17th century as the final and unique standard by which works of literature must be judged.

The University of North Carolina

[1] Charles Sorel, *Bibliothèque françoise* (Paris: Compaignie des Libraires du Palais, 1664).

[2] Lettre No. 414 (A André Falconet) in the J. H. Réveillé-Parise edition of the *Lettres de Gui Patin* (Paris: Baillière, 1846), III, 17-18.

[3] A. Furetière, *Le roman bourgeois* (Paris: Garnier, s.d.), pp. 212-13.

[4] Pp. 349-69. All references are to the original edition (mentioned in note 1, above).

[5] *Ibid.*, pp. 369-85.

[6] *Ibid.*, "Avant-Propos," pp. vi-vii.

[7] *Ibid.*, "Avant-Propos," pp. vi-vii.

[8] *Ibid.*, pp. 1-14. Chap. Ier: "Des livres qui traitent de la pureté de la langue françoise."

[9] *Ibid.*, p. 18.

[10] *Ibid.*, pp. 46-52, Chap. V: "Des livres qui traitent des mœurs."

[11] *Ibid.*, p. 168.

[12] *Ibid.*, p. 192.

[13] *Ibid.*, p. 184.

Louisiana-French Loan Words for 'Water-Fowl' in the Spanish Of St. Bernard Parish, Louisiana

LOUISIANA-FRENCH LOAN WORDS FOR 'WATER-FOWL' IN THE SPANISH OF ST. BERNARD PARISH, LOUISIANA

Raymond R. MacCurdy

In 1778, during the period of the Spanish regime in Louisiana, Governor Bernardo Gálvez established a colony of Spanish immigrants on Bayou Terre-aux-Boeufs, approximately twenty-five miles south of New Orleans and within the boundaries of present-day St. Bernard Parish. The descendents of the original colonists are called "Islanders," from Spanish *isleños*. Spanish is still the primary language of the towns of Delacroix, Reggio, Yscloskey, and to a lesser extent of Shell Beach and other communities; however, the great majority of the inhabitants are now perfectly bilingual in Spanish and English, and a few also speak Louisiana-French.

Whereas in the other Spanish colonies established during the Spanish regime the Spanish language eventually gave way, with few exceptions,[1] to the predominance of French and English, the *isleños* of St. Bernard managed to preserve their language, though not without its having been deeply affected by the surrounding French. Many French words entered into the Spanish lexicon, especially words for flora and fauna which were not known to the early Spanish settlers. Mostly fishermen, hunters, and trappers by trade, the *isleños* felt the need for a greater variety of words to designate the species of wild-life they encountered; hence, they naturally availed themselves of the established Louisiana-French terms. Words for the various species of water-fowl constitute a noteworthy example of these borrowings.

In the process of the adoption of French loan words, three practices may be observed: (1) the hispanization of the French word, by far the most common practice; (2) the literal translation into Spanish of the French term; and (3) the retention of the French pronunciation of the world. In the following list, the Spanish word is given first; the French or Louisiana-French source[2] is given in brackets; and the species is designated by the Latin term, followed by the English name. Abbreviations used are: *m.* (masculine), *f.* (feminine), La. (Lousiana), and Fr. (French).

barioneta, *f.* [La. Fr. *marionette.*] *Charitonetta albeola* L. Bufflehead Duck, called also the Butterball. The St. Bernard word is also pronounced *marioneta*.

becasina, *f.* [Fr. and La. Fr. *bécassine.*] *Gallinago delicata* Ord. Snipe. The St. Bernard term also designates a similar species in Argentina and the Antilles.³

becsí, *m.* [La. Fr. *bec-scie.*] *Mergus americanus* Cass. American Merganser, popularity called the Saw-bill Duck since the teeth in its bill resemble the edge of a saw. This duck is also called *moñito criollo, infra.*

becsí de mar, *m.* [La. Fr. *bec-scie de mer.*] *Mergus serrator* L. Spanish Drake, called also the Fish Duck.

bicuena, *f.* [La. Fr. *micoine.*] *Spatula clypeata* L. Shoveller, often called the Spoonbill Duck. Read traces the origin of the La. Fr. word to Algonquian.⁴

bransí, *m.* [La. Fr. *canard branchu.*] *Aix sponsa* L. Wood Duck, sometimes called the Summer Duck. This duck is known also by the Spanish name *pato de monte, infra.*

canar francés, *m.* [La. Fr. *canard français.*] *Anas platyrhynchos* L. Greenhead Mallard, commonly called the French Duck in English.

canar gris, *m.* [La. Fr. *canard gris.*] *Chaulelasmus streperus* L. Gadwall (duck).

canar nuar, *m.* [La. Fr. *canard noir.*] *Marila collaris* Donov. Black Jack, also called the Ring-necked Duck. More commonly called the *pato negro* in St. Bernard.

canar nuar de verano, *m.* [La. Fr. *canard noir d'été.*] *Anas fulvigula* Ridgw. Florida Duck, popularly called the Black Mallard. The Spanish terms *pato negro de verano* and *pato de isla* are more commonly used to designate this duck in St. Bernard.

congó, *m.* [La. Fr. *congo.*] *Nettion carolinense* Gmel. Green-winged Teal. This term is attributed to the color of the duck's crest or to the black spots on its underparts.⁵ It is also called the *pretañera de invierno, infra.*

dende, *m.* [La. Fr. *canard d' Inde,* Muscovy Duck.] *Clangula clangula americana* Bonap. American Golden-eye Duck, commonly known as the Whistler. Apparently the Spanish term was borrowed from La. Fr. *canard d' Inde* (*Cairina moschata* L.) and erroneously applied to the Golden-eye.

dogrí, *m.* [La. Fr. *deau gris.*] *Marila valisineria* Wils. Canvas-back Duck, also called the Horse Duck. It is known as the *canard cheval* in La. Fr. and *pato caballo* in St. Bernard Spanish.

egreta, *f*. [Fr. *aigrette*.] *Hydranassa tricolor ruficollis* Gosse. Louisiana Heron, generally called the Blue Crane.

egreta azur, *f*. [La. Fr. *aigrette bleue*.] *Florida caerulea caerulea* L. Little Blue Heron or Blue Egret.

macrela, *f*. [La. Fr. *macreuse?*] *Podilymbus podiceps* L. Pied-billed Grebe, popularly called the Hell-diver.

marioneta, *f*. Buffle-head Duck. See *barioneta, supra*.

moñito criollo, *m*. [*Sp. moño*, egret.] American Merganser. Also called *becsí, supra*.

otoñera, *f*. [La. Fr. *sarcelle printanière*.] *Querquedula discors* L. Blue-winged Teal. See *pretañera de verano, infra*.

pato caballo, *m*. [La. Fr. *canard cheval*.] Canvas-back Duck, Horse Duck. See *dogrí, supra*.

pato de isla, *m*. [La. Fr. *canard d'île*.] See *canar nuar de verano, supra*.

pato de monte, *m*. Wood Duck. See *bransí, supra*.

pato francés, *m*. Greenhead Mallard. See *canar francés, supra*.

pato mexicano, *m*. [*La. Fr. mexicain*.] *Dendrocygna fulva* Gmel. Fulvous Tree Duck.

pato negro, *m*. Black Jack Duck. See *canar nuar, supra*.

pato negro de verano, *m*. Florida Duck. See *canar nuar de verano, supra*.

payankí, *m*. [La. Fr. *paille-en-queue*.] *Dafila acuta* L. Pintail Duck, known also as the Sprig or Sprig-tail.

pretañera de invierno, *f*. [La. Fr. *sarcelle printanière* and *sarcelle d' hiver*.] *Nettion carolinense* Gmel. Green-winged Teal, also called Winter Teal or Northern Teal. The Spanish name for this duck is a confusion of the La. Fr. terms *sarcelle printanière*, Spring Teal, and *sarcelle d' hiver*, Winter Teal. Other Spanish names for this same species are *sarcela de invierno* and *sarcela de norte, infra*, and *congó, supra*.

pretañera de verano, *f*. [La. Fr. *sarcelle printanière* and *sarcelle d' été*.] *Querquedula discors* L. Blue-winged Teal. In spring, when this duck is in full plumage, it is called Spring Teal. In autumn, when it loses its plumage, it is called Autumn Teal, hence the Spanish name *otoñera* (from La. Fr. *sarcelle automnière*), *supra*. The Blue-winged Teal is said to have received these two names because it arrives in the fall and remains until late in the spring.[6] Those members of the species which remain through the summer are known as *sarcelas de verano, infra*.

puldó, *m*. [La. Fr. *poule d' eau*.] *Fulia americana* Gmel. Coot.

English-speaking natives of Louisiana also use the term *poule d' eau* for this bird.

rala, *f.* [Fr. and La. *râle.*] Rail, Marsh Hen. The St. Bernard word as well as the La. Fr. is applied indiscriminately to various species of rail and gallinule, including the Sora Rail (*Porzana carolina* L.), the Louisiana Clapper Rail (*Rallus crepitans saturatus* Hensh.), the King Rail (*Rallus elegans* Aud.), the Purple Gallinule (*Ionorsis martinicus* L.), and the Florida Gallinule (*Gallinula galeata galeata* L.).

sarcela, *f.* [Fr. *sarcelle.*] 1. *Querquedula discors* L. Blue-winged Teal; also called *sarcela de verano* and *pretañera de verano*, *supra*.

2. The generic term designating all species of Teal (family *Nettion* and *Querquedula*).

sarcela de invierno, *f.* Green-winged Teal. See *pretañera de invierno*, *supra*.

sarcela de norte, *f.* Green-winged Teal, also called *pretañera de verano* or simply *sarcela*, *supra*.

zenzen, *m.* [La. Fr. *zenzen.*[7]] *Mareca americana* L. Baldpate Duck. This word is pronounced in French fashion.

The University of New Mexico

---

[1] The exceptions apply to the few score descendants of the original settlers of Valenzuela, in present-day Assumption Parish, which was established also in 1778 by immigrants from the Canary Islands. The few remaining Spanish-speaking persons reside in several small towns of Assumption and Ascension Parishes and in small rural communities called *brulis* (from Fr. *brûlé*, "burned," so-called because the thick underbrush and other vegetation was burned to clear the ground for agricultural purposes). In contrast to the flourishing state of Spanish in the thriving communities of St. Bernard Parish, the language is rapidly dying out in Ascension and Assumption Parishes. Hardly any children speak it.

[2] Unless otherwise designated, the authority for all La. Fr. words cited is William A. Read, *Louisiana-French* (Louisiana State University Studies No. 5; Baton Rouge: Louisiana State University Press, 1931).

[3] Francisco J. Santamaría, *Diccionario general de americanismos* (3 vols.; Mexico: Editorial Pedro Robredo, 1942), I, 198.

[4] Read, *op. cit.*, pp. 96-97.

[5] *Ibid.*, p. 68.

[6] *Ibid.*

[7] Professor John Guilbeau, an authority on La. Fr., has furnished the information that *zenzen* designates the Baldpate Duck.

The Use of *Vos* in Panamanian Spanish

THE USE OF *VOS* IN PANAMANIAN SPANISH
Stanley L. Robe

Spanish-speaking colonists who came to the New World brought with them two familiar forms of address corresponding to the second person singular. In sixteenth century Spain *tú* was in ascendancy over *vos*, a form which was then used by the populace and has since practically disappeared in the peninsula. In America, however, *vos* found conditions favorable for its usage and flourished in areas where an intellectual tradition was slow in becoming established. Elsewhere the use of *tú* prevailed, as in Peru, Mexico, and Santo Domingo.

Two scholars have made excellent surveys of the use of *tú* and *vos* in America, Eleuterio F. Tiscornia in *La lengua de "Martín Fierro,"*[1] and Charles E. Kany in his *American-Spanish Syntax*.[2] Tiscornia scarcely mentions the use of *vos* in Panamanian Spanish (p. 135), while Kany cites examples (p. 81) taken from Narciso Garay's *Tradiciones y cantares de Panamá*[3] and from *Sangre criollo*, a collection of stories by Nacho Valdé.[4]

A somewhat misleading statement appears in Miguel Amado's "El lenguaje en Panamá."[5] After indicating the influence of Santo Domingo and Mexico and later Peru on the culture of the isthmus, on p. 642 Amado says of Panamanian speech:

> Característico es el empleo del *tú* pronominal y de las inflexiones del verbo que le corresponden, tal como en Perú, en Santo Domingo y en México, mientras en las regiones de América más apartadas de los centros de cultura se impone el *vos* con el consiguiente desgreño de las formas verbales.

While it is true that *tú* is the preferred familiar form of address in Panamanian Spanish, Amado makes no mention whatever of the existence of the *voseo* in the country. The remarks which follow will attempt to indicate more precisely the usage of *tú* and *vos* in Panama, an area in which this phenomenon has not been described adequately.

Kany remarks (p. 81) that the *vos* is used in the interior, particularly in the area adjoining Colombia. The present writer failed to observe it during a residence of several months near Pito and Permé, villages on the Atlantic coast within fifteen miles of the Colombian border, nor during a much shorter stay on the Pacific coast of the province of Darién in eastern Panama. It is probably little used in the northwestern province of Bocas del Toro, where English is spoken almost exclusively. The greatest use of the *voseo* is found in the area along the Pacific coast to the west of the Canal Zone, in the four central provinces of Coclé, Herrera, Los Santos, and Veraguas and also the province of Chiriquí.

Prof. Feliciano Quirós, formerly sub-director of the Juan D. Arosemena Normal School at Santiago, Veraguas province, and one of the few Panamanians of the interior who have studied the area's language, remarked to me verbally that the *voseo* is to be found more frequently in the mountainous areas of the interior where the Indian element of the population is more apparent. The *voseo*, he states, is not generally used in the *llanos* along the coast and is found least in those communities where there is a negro element in the population, as in Antón, Natá, and Santa María. In generally, Quirós' observation has been confirmed, although I have heard it in the provinces of Los Santos, Coclé, and Veraguas in areas which are not in the uplands of the interior.

Personal observation has shown that the *voseo* is confined to areas which are definitely rural, although occasionally it is used by the poorer class of residents in the smaller villages. Among the middle class in the towns *tú* is used exclusively. The latter usage is the only one heard in the urban areas of Panama and Colon.

Vos is used in informal speech in similar circumstances to those in which *tú* is found. In the family it is used by elders in addressing children. The latter do not generally speak to parents or grandparents by using the familiar form. *Vos* is also used among close friends or associates and occasionally is employed to address social inferiors.

In Panama the value of *vos* is singular. In the plural *ustedes* and its corresponding oblique forms are regularly employed. Garay (p. 162) comments on this practice: "Obsérvese como incurre el pueblo liberal del Istmo en la inveterada práctica americana de interpelar a sus copartidarios usando de la tercera persona del plural en vez de la segunda."

One must note that in Panama the *o* of *vos* is pronounced with a somewhat open timbre while the *s* is aspirated in final position or when a voiceless consonant follows. The final *s* of the verbal endings receives a similar treatment. This practice accounts for the spellings employed by Panamanian writers in the examples which follow. Inasmuch as the *voseo* is not a problem of morphology alone, its various aspects in both pronominal and verbal use will be considered. Consequently much of the significance of the following description stems from the combinations of the familiar pronouns and their accompanying verb forms.

Both *tú* and *vos* are used as nominative pronouns. The former is employed exclusively in the towns and cities and is even preferred in rural areas where *vos* is also observed, as the following examples will indicate. The following are from the provinces of Coclé and Veraguas; *tú podéis, tú coméis, tú sabéis, tú tenés, tú veis* (*vais*). In Coclé and Los Santos were heard *vos tenéis, vos sabéis,* and *decíme vos.* Writers who describe life in the central provinces of Panama confirm this observation, *tú no merecei, tú no te atrevei;*[6] yet there are frequent uses of *vos,* as *vos sabes, a mí no me puedes engañar vos,*[7] *¿y vos de onde venís?*[8]

One finds *te* used as an accusative in the speech of those who ordinarily use *vos: te pilló con ese madito bicho,*[9] *no te pensés que ta teniéndote alzao aquí pa bonito.*[10] The same usage occurs in the dative: *te juro* (Verbel, p. 62), *pa decirte si serás flojo* (Riera, p. 4), *que te sepa hacer aprecio* (Valdés, p. 15).

Rural speakers prefer *tu* as a possessive: *pa vos y tu hermano* (Valdés, pp. 14-15), *se manche con tu sangre maldita* (Castillo, p. 21).

As a reflexive *te* is also preferred: *tú no te atrevei* (Castillo, p. 96), *y ahora te vai* (Castillo, p. 22), *pa que así no te podáis valé* (Verbel, p. 62), *te quemáis* (Garay, p. 41). One author, however, uses the plural *os,* which has not been observed elsewhere: *os casaréis* (Valdés, p. 14).

Only as an object of a preposition is *vos* used obliquely: *pa vos y tu hermano* (Valdés, pp. 14-15), *trabajando pa vos y los hijos, voy hacé un buen escarmiento con vos y él* (Verbel, p. 62). Verbel, however, (p. 62) also uses *ti* as a prepositional object, as *y a ti te voy a escuerá las patas.* Among rural residents of the province of Veraguas *ti* is regarded as offensive and is hence avoided. Thus one hears *¿qué te pasa a tú?*, in which *tú* replaces the terminal form of the pronoun. However, when an offensive meaning is desired, *ti* can be attributed a nominative value, as *¡más cholo feo seis ti!,* also heard in Veraguas.

The verb forms used with *vos* are usually those corresponding to the standard second person plural, although singular forms occasionally accompany it. More frequently the plural verb form accompanies the singular *tú.* The following usages of the present indicative were observed personally in the central provinces: *tú podéis, tú coméis, tú sabéis, vos tenéis, seis ti, tú veis,* and *vais, decís, salís,* used without pronominal forms. Panamanian authors of literature set in the central provinces and Chiriquí give abundant testimony of the confusion of pronouns and verb forms: *tú no merecei* (Castillo, p. 21), *tú no te atrevei* (Castillo, p. 96), *vos no sois* (Riera, p. 4), *tenéis vos* (Riera, p. 5), *no me puedes engañar vos* (Valdés, p. 14), *vos sabes* (Valdés, ibid.), *¿y qué vais a hacel aúra?* (Cajar Escala, p. 36), *de onde venís*, Cajar Escala, p. 38). One formation ends in *-és, tú tenés,* heard in El Embalsadero, Veraguas. However, the endings *-áis, -éis* and *-ís* are those most frequently employed.

A similar preference is observed in the present subjunctive. Observed personally were *tú habléis, procedáis,* while the following are from Panamanian authors: *no creai, no tengai miedo* (Castillo, p. 21), *no llores mujer* (Riera, p. 4), *no seáis entrometío* (Riera, p. 5). One author, however, uses a form ending in *-és: no te pensés* (Riera, p. 4).

The ending *-eis* is not popular in the preterite. Only one occurrence has been noted: *Oye, Voj, cuándo llegasteis.*[11] Generally preferred are the archaic forms of the second person plural ending in *-stes: hicistes, luchastes, sostuvistes, convidastes, arrojastes,* all observed personally in the central provinces. Narciso Garay (p. 109), cites this usage as persisting in Panama in spite of the efforts of educators to eradicate it.

Imperative forms corresponding to both the singular and plural are employed, although only a singular meaning is attributed to them. Quirós says in *El castellano en Panamá*s Fonología (p. 5): ". . . .pues ni siquiera usamos el imperativo en forma plural. Para tal mandato usamos *vayan.*"[12] The following uses are from native speakers in the central provinces: *venid, ven, ten, contestadme, decíme vos, traéme.* Panamanian authors of works set in the central provinces supply the following: *si no jacei na dame acá tus pantalones* (Castillo, p. 97), *Oye, Voj* (Carles, op. cit.), *repara en mis canas* (Valdés, p. 15), *vení* (Riera, p. 4). Quirós (p. 1) cites the forms *cantá, cogé, subi* as being from the province of Los Santos, adding that "estos usos son exclusivamente vulgares."

In the imperfect indicative one hears usually those forms normally used with *tú: que vos si eras hombre* (Riera, p. 4). Only one example has been observed of the use of *voseo* in the future: *volverá a ti y os casaréis* (Valdés, pp. 13-14). In some cases a periphrastic construction replaces the future: *¿qué vais a hacel aúra?* (Cajar Escala, p. 36). The only usage observed of the imperfect subjunctive indicates that the third person singular verb form may even be used: *Y vos Manolo hacé como si juera yo* (Riera, p. 4).

The above observations indicate that both *tú* and *vos* are used in Panama. In the cities and towns *tú* and its corresponding verb forms are used exclusively. *Vos* is used by only a segment of the population, being confined to rural areas; but even there it shares many of its functions with *tú*. As a pronoun, the use of *vos* is somewhat restricted. It appears in the nominative, although, at least in the central provinces, *tú* is employed more frequently in such a position. Again it appears as the object of a preposition, perhaps due to the offensive connotation ascribed to *ti*, although this usage is not exclusive. Elsewhere the singular pronoun is used almost without exception.

The standard forms of the familiar second person plural are those preferred in verbs. The singular form occasionally accompanies the nominative *vos*, as *vos sabes*, but more frequently the plural verb accompanies the nominative singular *tú*, as *tú sabéis*. In a few cases the archaic ending *-és* is preserved in the present indicative or subjunctive, as *tenés*, *pensés*. The preterite regularly retains the archaic ending *-stes*. One notes then that in Panamanian speech the *voseo* shows a much greater degree of persistence in the verb system than in pronominal use.

Although the area under treatment is relatively small, the writer hopes that this description of a specific phenomenon will be a modest contribution toward completing our knowledge of its geography in American Spanish.

The University of California at Los Angeles

---

[1] *Biblioteca de dialectología hispanoamericana*, III (Buenos Aires, 1930), pp. 120-37. The article of Ira E. Chart, "The 'voseo' and 'tuteo' in America" (*Modern Language Forum*, XXVIII [1943], 17-24), is based largely upon material drawn from Tiscornia's treatment.

[2] Chicago, 1945, pp. 55-91.

[3] Brussels, 1930.

[4] Panama, 1943.

[5] *Boletín de la Academia Argentina de Letras*, XIV (1945), 641-66.

[6] Moisés Castillo, *Allá onde uno*, Panama, 1946, pp. 21, 96.

[7] Ignacio de J. Valdés, Jr., *Cuentos panameños de la ciudad y del campo* (Panama, 1928), p. 14.

[8] José A. Cajar Escala, *El cabecilla* (Panamá, 1945), p. 38.

[9] Mauricio Verbel, "El buchí," *repertorio Americano* (San José, Costa Rica), XLV, No. 4, p. 62. This story is set in Chiriquí province.

[10] Ariel Doroaf [Adolfo Riera], "El trapiche avisa," *El veragüense* (Santiago de Veraguas), January 16, 1944, p. 4.

[11] Rubén D. arles, "La gente de 'allá abajo,' " *La Estrella de Panamá* (Panama), July 16, 1945.

[12] Santiago de Veraguas, 1941, 12 pp. mimeographed.

Preconception of Reality, and Abulia, in Nineteenth-century French Decadent Literature

PRECONCEPTION OF REALITY, AND ABULIA, IN NINETEENTH-CENTURY FRENCH DECADENT LITERATURE

James M. Smith

By *Decadent* we refer here to those writers, especially the ones of the latter half of the century, beginning notably with Baudelaire, who rebelled against the bourgeois society that produced them, reacting against and most often inverting its social, moral, and aesthetic bases. In this study we are concerned with their reaction against the bourgeois concept of man's place in society. Man, we are told, is instinctively a gregarious animal. The Decadent is usually just the contrary, avoiding contact with his fellow man, carefully cultivating his solitude. Unwilling or unable to face the world in which he lives, he often retires into an ideal world of his own creation, there to lead a life of his own choice. Among the decadents who thus seek refuge in the world of fancy, thought comes to take the place of action, both in the writers themselves and in their heroes. The figure of Hamlet, as the archetype of the man too engrossed in speculation to act, hovers over this whole age.

Among the writers of the period it is Remy de Gourmont who sums up the problem most succinctly: " . . . Si une trop grande partie de la sensibilité se transforme en intelligence, la vie est définitivement vaincue."[1] Baudelaire contrasts the spontaneity of children with the lack of it in men who think too much:

> Avec cette admirable et lumineuse promptitude qui caractérise les enfants, chez qui le désir, la délibération et l'action ne font, pour ainsi dire, qu'une seule faculté, par laquelle ils se distinguent des hommes dégénérés, en qui, au contraire, la délibération mange presque tout le temps . . . .[2]

In Gourmont's *Sixtine,* we find:

> Le monde matériel et inconscient ne vit et ne se meut que dans l'intelligence qui le perçoit et le récrée à nouveau selon des formes personnelles . . . Le monde idéal, tel qu'il [Des Entragues, le héros] le détenait, suffisait à son activité toute mentale et trop inerme pour la lutte.[3]

The leading character of Gourmont's *Le fantôme* is of the same mould as the hero of *Sixtine*: " . . . Arrivé à cet état mental, l'homme a compris l'inutilité absolue du mouvement,[4] il se confine en lui-même, se trouve enfin apte à la seule pensée . . . ." "Agir et penser sont des contraires qui ne s'identifient que dans l'Absolu."[5] In Joséphin Péladan's *Le vice suprême*, at a banquet à la Sade, where each of the guests recounts what he knows of the week's evil, one of those present comments, rather sadly: "Aujourd'hui le bien et le mal ne se font plus, ils se parlent. L'action est morte."[6] André Gide prefers motivating action in others to acting himself: "J'aime mieux faire agir que d'agir."[7] And, across the Channel, Walter Pater urged a life of "being rather than doing."[8]

The key to much of this life of non-action lies in the tendency of the Decadents to conceive in advance an idea of life which their actual experiences later proved to be false. Upon leaving the world of chimeras which they had fashioned for themselves, they were disillusioned and in their disillusionment frequently turned inward again. Their wills already weakened by introspection, they were incapable of making the necessary adjustments to adapt themselves to the world as they actually found it. "Les Adolphes—pour généraliser le nom du type le plus caractérisé de l'espèce—sont comme des Narcisses de leur propre misère, toujours en train de suivre leur agonie dans le miroir que leur offre leur analyse, et cependant ils meurent vraiment."[9]

Gérard de Nerval was disappointed upon seeing the foreign lands that he visited, for they did not live up to the preconceived idea he had fashioned of them: "Ainsi, pour moi, déjà bien des contrées du monde se sont réalisées et le souvenir qu'elles m'ont laissé est loin d'égaler les splendeurs du rêve qu'elles m'ont fait perdre."[10] Some of the leading characters of Flaubert show this trait.[11] Emma Bovary, having filled her mind with romantic fancies during her surreptitious reading at the convent school, is dissatisfied with the life of a bourgeoise. Later in her adulterous career, when she seeks happiness in her illicit love affair with the petty clerk Léon, she finds that the actual joys of extra-marital love are not nearly so intense as she had imagined them (her earlier love affair with Rodolphe had disillusioned her in her partner but not in *love*): "Elle se promettait continuellement, pour son prochain voyage, une félicité profonde, puis elle s'avouait ne rien sentir d'extraordinaire."[12] For his part, Léon is more attracted by the very idea of having a mistress than by Emma as a person. During the first part of their liaison he sees her as "l'amoureuse de tous les romans, l'héroïne de tous les drames, le vague *elle* de tous les volumes de vers."[13] Later Emma becomes more and more demanding and less attractive, and Léon refuses to sacrifice himself to save her from bankruptcy, shame and ultimate death. Both of them, mediocre creatures at best, seek to find in illicit love the fulfillment of desires far beyond their potentialities, awakened in them by their earlier readings.

In *Salammbô*, the heroine is consumed with a desire to see the sacred veil of Tanit, the moon goddess. She has forged in advance an idea of the veil and upon seeing it feels a certain disappointment: ". . . Quand elle l'eut bien contemplé, elle fut surprise de ne pas avoir ce bonheur qu'elle s'imaginait autrefois. Elle restait mélancolique devant son rêve accompli."[14]

In Edouard Rod's *Les trois coeurs*, Richard leaves his wife for his mistress. He is soon disappointed in the latter, for she does not resemble Cleopatra—she has none of the traits of the great mistresses of history. Essentially the same situation is found in Adrien Remacle's *L'absente*. In the *Aphrodite* of Pierre Louys, the sculptor Demetrios finds that the charms of the queen can not compete successfully with those of the idealized statue he has made of her: "Quand il revit la reine elle-même, il la trouva dépouillée de tout ce qui avait son charme."[15]

As a result of this preconception of reality Decadent heroes often find themselves incapable of action when confronted with situations demanding it. Flaubert's Frédéric Moreau, hero of the *Education sentimentale*, nourished in his youth on romantic novels and verse, works out carefully in advance what he will do and say in the presence of his lady, but when the actual occasion presents itself he is incapable of either speech or action. The hero of Edouard Dujardin's *Les lauriers sont coupés* resembles Frédéric Moreau, working out in advance speeches to make to his sweetheart and then not being able to recite them when the time comes:

> '—Mon amie, j'ai songé aux choses qui sont entre nous; follement je vous désirais; que ce soit mon excuse; je vous ai contrainte; j'implore votre pardon. Je puis rester ici cette nuit, mon amie . . . Adieu! vous êtes bien aimée; je vous rends votre corps, et je vous quitte, parce que je vous aime.—Et je prendrai sa tête dans mes mains, je regarderai ses yeux, et je baiserai ses levres.—Adieu.'
>
> Qui, ces paroles . . . Et jamais je n'ai eu l'occasion, ces paroles, de les dire. [Then, at a later visit with his sweetheart, the hero muses:]
>
> . . . Il est temps de partir. Je n'ai pas écrit ce que je projetais de dire; bah! bien inutile; je me souviendrai; j'ai d'ailleurs le papier d'il y a un mois [cf. *supra*].[16]

The outstanding treatment of this theme among the Decadents is to be found, perhaps, in Gourmont's *Sixtine: roman de la vie cérébrale*. Here again we see the failure of the thinker when faced with the necessity of action. Hubert Des Entragues, the hero, fails in pursuit of Sixtine because his constant self-analysis has weakened his will to act. Sixtine wants to be taken. Hubert, his vitality all but destroyed, never rises to the occasion:

> Sitôt en présence de *Sixtine*, Hubert sentit tout son plaisir gâté par les points d'interrogation qu'un schéma algébrique avait posés, non résolus. De même sa volonté d'agir faiblissait sous le poids du présent.[17]

Many of these introverts show themselves inept to experience genuine emotions. Des Entragues says:

> Je ne sais pas vivre. Perpétuelle cérébration, mon existence est la négation même de la vie ordinaire, faite d'ordinaires amours.
> Je suis en train de vivre et je ne sais comment m'y prendre.[18]

The Goncourts' Charles Demailly, a writer, like Des Entragues, suffers also from having speculated too much: ". . . L'amour de Charles . . . etait un amour de tête. Il aimait peut-être plus encore en auteur qu'en amoureux."[19] Mérodack, the *mage* of Péladan's *Le vice suprême*, finds himself equally incapable of feeling a genuine amorous passon: "J'ai le coeur à la tête, je suis le fiancé des idées, un chevalier de Malte du Mystère. J'ai trop dépouillé de l'homme pour m'absorber en une passion."[20] As in a great many of these figures, the incapacity for action of Mérodack comes from his having read too much: "Avant d'apercevoir le sphinx de l'initiation, il s'était jeté dans une lecture, à esprit perdu. . . . Le livre lui gâta la vie."[21]

Because of this hypercerebration these figures suffer from exhaustion and disillusionment even before experiencing reality. In Huysmans' *Là-Bas*, Durtal, still another fictional author,

> manquait d'appétit, n'était réellement tourmenté que par l'éréthéisme de sa cervelle. Il était usé de corps, élimé d'âme, inapte à aimer, las des tendresses avant même qu'il ne les reçût et si dégoûté après qu'il les avait subies . . . Puis, quelle maladie que celle-là: se souiller d'avance par la réflexion tous les plaisirs . . . .[22]

In Maurice Barrès' novel *Sous l'oeil des barbares*, called by its author a "roman de la vie intérieure," the hero "eut des lectures qui lui donnèrent sur les choses des certitudes hâtives et pleines d'âcreté."[23] He is analyzed by his *amie*: "—Ah! tu sais trop de choses avant les initiations. Je pense que tu écoutes ce qui monte du passé, et les morts t'auront mangé le coeur." Philippe replies: "Mais vois donc que je suis las, las avant l'effort . . ."[24] And in Marcel Schwob we find: "Nous étions arrivés dans un temps extraordinaire où les romanciers nous avaient montré toutes les faces de la vie humaine et tous les dessous des pensées. On était lassé de bien des sentiments avant de les avoir éprouvés...."[25]

This state of abulia, most often the consequence of departing from reality too far and too long, becomes chronic in the Decadents. In these beings, in whom almost all activity is limited to the mind, life itself is almost extinct. The hero of Barrès' *Le culte du moi*, another victim of unwholesome introspection, declares: "... Je n'ai plus le désir ni la volonté de manifester rien qui soit digne de moi. L'effort égoïste et âpre m'a stérilisé." "Je n'ai plus d'énergie...."[16] Philippe remarks, with a certain note of regret for the healthy animal activity of ordinary men: "C'est le secret de la vie que trouve spontanément la foule."[27]

In Huysmans' novel *A rebours*, Des Esseintes, its hero, presents one of the more striking examples of abulia to be found in Decadent literature. Like many of his contemporaries, both real and fictive, he hates movement, preferring to travel by means of his imagination. Once, when he does venture out from his fantastic retreat—in which the dining-room is fitted up to resemble a ship's salon, even to a coil of rope which gives the air a marine flavor—with the intention of going to England, he finds that he lacks the will power to carry out his plans and hastily returns to the comforts of home and artifice.

In "Le bonheur," of Henri de Régnier, the writer gives a poetic description of satiety and abulia:

> Aussi bien que les pleurs le rire fait des rides;
> Ne dis jamais: Encore, et dis plutôt: Assez ...
> Le Bonheur est un Dieu qui marche les mains vides
> Et regarde la Vie avec des yeux baissés.[28]

A somewhat similar description is found in Flaubert's *Tentation de Saint Antoine*: "... Point de dérangement et point de travail! —La tête le plus bas possible, c'est le secret du bonheur!"[29]

According to Bourget, the weakening of the will became such a general phenomenon that all writers preoccupied with exactitude observed it: "C'est devenu le thème habituel de l'école dite naturaliste...."[30] Zola shows individuals incapable of surmounting their environment, Daudet those incapable of surmounting their sensations, Huysmans and Paul Alexis weak creatures lacking the will to act. Edouard Rod may be added to the group. His Michel Teissier is incapable of overcoming his illicit passion, and, possessed of an active conscience, he suffers terrible remorse.[31]

This abulia may be traced ultimately to the overemphasis on the individual, one of the primary elements in Decadent literature. Through self-analysis Decadent individualism led to an escape from the world of reality into a world of fancy, undermined the ability to act, destroyed the will. Unlike the heroes of Romantic fiction, who, if melancholy, were for the most part dynamic, the typical Decadent heroes were reduced to a state of unwholesome, sterile introspection. Action was considered degrading.

Against a singularly rich background of palpitating jungle life, Leconte de Lisle projects a picture of "inaction surhumaine":

> Les Brahmanes muets et de longs jours chargés,
> Ensevelis vivants dans leurs songes austères . . .,
> Las des vaines rumeurs de l'homme et des cités,
> En un monde inconnu puisaient leurs voluptés.
> . . . Ils fixaient leur esprit sur l'Ame intérieure.[32]

In Flaubert's Saint Anthony, medieval asceticism is turned into a morbid cult of inactivity: "L'homme étant esprit, doit se retirer des choses mortelles. Toute action le dégrade. Je voudrais ne pas tenir à la terre,—même par la plante de mes pieds!"[33] Philippe, in Barrès' *Jardin de Bérénice*, says of his friend and councilor: "Pas un instant il n'admit que je fisse de l'action, au sens qu'ils opposent à contemplation."[34] Des Entragues shows this same scorn for action:

> Dans la sphère où il évoluait, tout lui appartenait: sous l'oeil de la logique, il était le maître absolu d'une réalité transcendante dont la domination pleine de joies ne lui laissait pas le loisir d'une vulgaire vie et de préoccupations humaines. Vouloir? Vouloir quoi? Ah! qu'il est bien plus intéressant de se regarder penser. . . .[35]

Gourmont's Diomède declares:

> Je veux jouer avec la vie, je veux passer en rêvant; je ne veux pas croire; je ne veux pas aimer; je ne veux pas souffrir; je ne veux pas être heureux; je ne veux pas être dupe. Je regarde, j'observe, je juge, je souris.[36]

Unsuited for the sterner realities of life by their intense introspection, the Decadents deliberately cultivated their abulia, scorning action and the real world—even life itself. Des Entragues declares: "La vie, je n'y tiens pas: si j'avais un doute à ce sujet, je me prouverais le contraire en la quittant."[37] *Axël*, of Villiers de l'Isle-Adam, stands as the most striking example of the undermining of the will to act, of the very will to live, by superrefinement of thought.[38] At the end of the play the hero states: "J'ai trop pensé pour daigner agir! . . . La seule fièvre dont il faille . . . nous guérir, est celle d'exister." "Vivre? les serviteurs feront cela pour nous."[39]

[1] *Promenades philosophiques, première série* (Paris: Mercure de France, 1916), p. 125.

[2] *L'art romantique* (Paris: Conard, 1925), p. 132. Paul Bourget brings up a similar problem in the field of creative writing, contrasting spontaneous inspiration and vicarious experience gained from secondary sources: "C'est par la critique ... que l'éducation de tout esprit commence aujourd'hui, puisque premier enseignement reçu est celui du travail des autres. .... L'analyse de la pensée de nos prédécesseurs précède la formation de notre propre pensée ... Ainsi la spontanéité irraisonnée qui animait, qui soutenait les premiers poètes devient-elle chez nous une exception de plus en plus rare. Nous avons des théories avant d'exécuter nos oeuvres, et c'est d'après ces théories que nous essayons de produire ces oeuvres. Est-il possible, dans des conditions pareilles, d'arriver à cette couleur de la vie, qui fut le privilège inné des artistes moins intellectuels que nous ne sommes, et surtout que ne seront nos successeurs? La réflexion ... ne répugne-t-elle point, par un antagonisme invincible, à la création?"—*Essais de psychologie contemporaine* (Paris: Plon, 1899), II, 107.

[3] *Sixtine* (Paris: Mercure de France, 1928), p. 136.

[4] Cf. Baudelaire: "Je hais le mouvement qui déplace les lignes," in "La beauté," *Les fleurs du mal*; also, "Les hiboux," *ibid*.

[5] *Le pèlerin du silence. Le fantôme* ... (Paris: Mercure de France, s.d.), pp. 45, 47.

[6] *Le vice suprême* (Paris: Librarie de la Presse, 1886), p. 174.

[7] *Conversation avec un Allemand quelques années avant la guerre*, quoted in Mario Praz, *The Romantic Agony* (London: Oxford University Press, 1933), p. 366.

[8] *Appreciations* (London: The MacMillan Library Edition, 1910), p. 61.

[9] Bourget, *op. cit.*, II, 251 (see, also, the essays on Flaubert and the Goncourts). Bourget considers Werther the first of these heroes in whom there is a conflict between "l'âme artificielle et l'action" (*loc. cit.*).

Cf. Rousseau, *Les confessions* (Paris: Garnier, s.d.), Part I, Bk. III, 96: "La prévoyance a toujours gâté chez moi la jouissance."

Sainte-Beuve points out the same trait in Chateaubriand's René: ". . . . Pour lui, il n'y a ni passions ni plaisirs; son analyse les a décomposés d'avance, sa précoce réflexion les a décolorés. Savoir trop tôt, savoir toutes choses avant de les sentir, c'est là le mal de certains hommes, de certaines générations presque entières, venues à un âge trop mûr de la société" (*Chateaubriand et son groupe littéraire* [Paris: Calmann-Lévy, 1889], I, 344-45).

[10] Quoted in Kléber Haedens, *Gérard de Nerval ou la sagesse romantique* (Paris: Grasset, 1939), p. 119.

[11] Cf. Bourget, *op. cit.*, I, 150 ff.

[12] *Madame Bovary* (Paris: Conard, 1930), p. 390.

[13] *Ibid.*, p. 367.

[14] *Salammbô* (Paris: Charpentier, 1911), p. 227.

[15] *Aphrodite* (Paris: Albin Michel, 1932), p. 39. In Remy de Gourmont's *Les chevaux de Diomède* (Paris: Mercure de France, s.d.), p. 181, Néobelle sighs, after yielding to Diomède's desires: "—Je regrette le songe que je me faisais de l'amour."

[16] *Les lauriers sout coupés* (Paris: Messein, 1924), pp. 70-71,75.

[17] P. 109.

[18] Pp. 34, 117.

[19] *Charles Demailly* (Paris: Flammarion et Fasquelle, s.d.), p. 197.
[20] P. 127.
[21] P. 12.
[22] *Là-Bas* (Paris: Crès, 1930), II, 51.
[23] *Sous l'oeil des barbares* (Paris: Plon, 1921), pp. 52, 64.
[24] *Ibid.*, pp. 96, 97. Paul Bourget (*op. cit.*, II, 248-49) sees this work as an example of the "dangereux abus de la littérature, ou mieux ... de la pensée." "Il [Barrès] devance l'expérience de la vie et il s'attribue les passions qu'il n'a pas éprouvées encore ...." The German polemicist Max Nordau considers Barrès as "the incarnation of the pure ego-mania of the incapacity of adaptation in the degenerate." (*Degeneration* [New York: Appleton & Co., 1895], p. 310.)
[25] "Les portes de l'opium," *Un coeur double* (Paris: Gallimard, 1921), p. 131.
[26] *Op cit.*, p. 277.
[27] *Le jardin de Bérénice* (Paris: Plon, 1921), p. 114. (*Le culte de moi* is a trilogy composed of *Sous l'oeil des barbares*, *Un homme libre* and *Le jardin de Bérénice*.)
[28] *Vestigia flammae* (Paris: Mercure de France, 1921).
[29] *La tentation de Saint Antoine* (Paris: Conard, 1924), p. 193.
[30] *Op. cit.*, II, 169.
[31] *La vie privée de Michel Teissier* (Paris: Michel Perrin, 1924).
[32] "Bhagavat," *Poèmes antiques* (Paris: Lemerre, s.d.).
[33] *Op. cit.*, p. 42.
[34] P. 119. In *Sous l'oeil des barbares* (p. 89), Philippe's master exclaims: "... Aspirer à quelque but! n'est-ce pas oublier la sagesse?" Philippe says himself (p. 160): "... J'ai appris ... qu'une belle pensée est préférable à une belle action."
[35] *Sixtine*, pp. 136-37.
[36] *Les chevaux de Diomède*, p. 34.
[37] *Sixtine*, p. 155.
[38] Cf. Rimbaud, "Chanson de la plus haute tour," *Illuminations* (Paris: Mercure de France, 1939):
> Par délicatesse
> J'ai perdu ma vie.

[39] *Axël* (Paris: Mercure de France, 1923), pp. 262, 261. Cf. the following passage attributed to Villiers by Arthur Symons in *The Symbolist Movement* (New York: E. P. Dutton and Co., 1919), p. 151: "As at a play, in a central stall, one sits out, so as not to disturb one's neighbors—out of courtesy, in a word—some play written in a wearisome style and of which one does not like the subject, so I lived, out of politeness: *je vivais par politesse.*"
There is a situation similar to that at the end of *Axël* in George Sand's *Indiana*, when Sir Ralph Brown speaks to Indiana of suicide, after finding supreme happiness with her:

" '... Le premier rayon de pourpre qui tomba sur le bosquet d'orangers m'y trouva à genoux et bénissant Dieu.

" 'Ne croyez pourtant pas que j'acceptai tout d'un coup le bonheur inespéré qui venait de renouveler ma destinée. J'eus peur de mesurer l'avenir radieux qui se levait sur moi, et, lorsque Indiana souleva ses paupières pour me sourire, je lui montrai la cascade et lui parlai de mourir.

" 'Si vous ne regrettez pas d'avoir vécu jusqu'à ce matin, lui dis-je, nous pouvons affirmer l'un et l'autre que nous avons goûté le bonheur dans la plénitude; et c'est une raison de plus pour quitter la vie, car mon astre pâlirait peut-être demain.' " —*Indiana* (Paris: Calmann-Lévy, s.d.), p. 350.

Sir Ralph and Indiana do not carry out their suicidal intent, however, while Axël erects a philosophical program out of his nihilism.

A Note on Scott in Spain

A NOTE ON SCOTT IN SPAIN
Sterling A. Stoudemire

In Spain, as in all European countries, the novels and narrative poems of Sir Walter Scott were of great significance and influence in introducing themes and techniques dear to the heart of the Romantics. It is most likely that among Spaniards Scott first came to the attention of the *emigrados* who were living in London at the time of the first publication of many of his works; somewhat later Scott came to be known and read in Spain in French translations and in Italian translations.[1] The first translation into Spanish of Scott's novels (*Ivanhoe* and *The Talisman*) appeared in London in 1825; the first translation to be published in Spain (*The Talisman*) appeared in Barcelona in 1826.[2] It is worthy of note that the first translations in Spain were published by the progressive and international-minded Catalans who were to introduce into the Peninsula the works of many foreigns authors, especially those of France, Germany, and Italy. Soon the Catalan interest in foreign literatures was picked up by all of Spain and Scott's novels and the works of others began to appear in several of the leading cities. The many translations of Scott's novels—single novels, collections, and even those advertised as "obras completas"—paralleled, in the main, the Romantic period in Spain, even though some titles continued to be published through most of the nineteenth century.

Several of Scott's novels were introduced into Spain in a form which is not discussed by Messrs. Churchman and Peers—the Italian opera. Also the study of Henry A. White[3] is far from complete in its consideration of this particular manifestation of Scott, and it fails to list the titles of some of the librettos which were derived from Scott's novels. It was in the same year as the first publication of a Scott novel in Spain—1826—that the Italian opera made one of its longest strides forward in its captivation and domination of the theater-going public of Madrid. The Italian opera had been popular in Spain for a long time; since the middle of the eighteenth century it had had some vogue.[4] The end of the eighteenth century saw a remarkable increase in favor of this art form in Spain, but the period of the Napoleonic occupation was marked by lassitude and apathy in most of the arts. About 1815 there began something of a rebirth in the opera as well as in the drama. On June 13, 1826, the performance of Rossini's *Zelmira* "... hizo estallar en el público, no ya un entusiasmo, sino un verdadero delirio, una fiebre, un fanatismo,"[5] which was to last on through the Romantic period and beyond. These operas certainly introduced into Spain much that was new in stage machinery, techniques, and themes from foreign literatures. The librettists seemed to take as their source materials almost everything on which they could lay their hands. Some of these innovations came to be a part of the stock materials of the Spanish Romantics, especially of the dramatists.[6]

At least six of Scott's works found their way to the hands of librettists writing for the Italian composers of the early nineteenth century: *The Lady of the Lake*, *The Betrothed*, *Kenilworth*, *Old Mortality*, *Ivanhoe*, and *The Bride of Lamermoor*.

La Donna del lago[7] (1819), by Gioachino Rossini and Leone Andrea Tottola, from Scott's narrative poem *The Lady of the Lake* (1810), was presented in Madrid at the Príncipe theater, July 25, 1828, two years before it was translated into Spanish as a *novela histórica*; it was repeated in the seasons of 1830 and 1837.

Il Contestabile di Chester, *El condestable de Chester*[8] (1829), by Giovanni Pacini and Domenico Gilardoni, from Scott's *The Betrothed* (1825), was presented in Madrid at the Príncipe theater, July 26, 1831. It was first translated into Spanish by Pedro Mata (Paris, 1840; Barcelona, 1842).

Il Castello di Kenilworth, *El castillo de Kenilworth*[9] by Gaetano Donizetti and Leone Andrea Tottola, from Scott's *Kenilworth* (1821), was presented in Madrid at the Cruz theater, October 17, 1835. A Spanish translation of the novel had already appeared in Valencia four years previously. *Elizabetta, Regina d'Inghilterra*, by Rossini and Schmith, is often listed as derived from the same source. The only flaw in this statement is that this opera was performed in Naples six years before Scott's *Kenilworth* was published.

I Puritani e I Cavalieri, *Los puritanos y los caballeros*[10] (1835), by Vincenzo Bellini and Carlo Pepoli, from Scott's *Old Mortality* (1816), was presented in Madrid at the Cruz theater, September 26, 1836. The earliest Spanish translation listed by Churchman and Peers, even though it is called *tercera edición*, is 1838. This was one of the most popular of all the Italian operas in Spain and continued to be sung almost every year on down beyond the middle of the century. It is still to be heard occasionally.

Lucia di Lamermoor[11] (1835) by Gaetano Donizetti and Salvatore Cammarano, from Scott's *The Bride of Lamermoor*

(1819), was presented in Madrid at the Cruz theater, August 2, 1837. A Spanish translation of the novel, *La pastora de Lamermoor o La desposada*, had appeared in 1828. *Lucia* was presented again in 1840 and since that time has remained a favorite in Spain as well as in many other parts of the world.

Il Templario[12] (1840), by Ottone Nicolai and Geronimo Maria Marini, from Scott's *Ivanhoe* (1819), was presented in Madrid at the Cruz theater, November 11, 1841, and was repeated in 1845. The novel had appeared in Spanish as early as 1825.

One of the chief contributions of the Italian opera to the Romantic drama was in the field of stage machinery and decoration. The opera and the drama were presented in the same theaters in Madrid, mainly the Cruz and the Príncipe, the opera with elaborate stage settings and scenery, the drama with the barest minimum of decoration. It is quite obvious that the pre-Romantics in Madrid did not have to search far in order to find the directions they needed to lead them to a full and elaborate use of scenery after 1834. Two of the operas in the decade before the Romantic era that contributed to that knowledge were *La Donna del lago* and *Il Contestabile di Chester*. The following descriptions will give a glimpse of the sort of thing that was found in the Italian opera, through which Scott indirectly made his contribution to the drama in Spain.

La Donna del lago:

> El teatro representa la famosa roca de Benledi, cubierta en su cumbre de espesos bosques, la que extendiéndose hacia abajo forma un dilatado valle en cuyo centro está el lago de Katrine, producido de las aguas que caen de la roca, y sobre el cual se verá un puente de troncos de árboles. (I, 1)
>
> Elena, en un barquichuelo en el lago. Llega a la orilla, salta en tierra y ata el barco a un tronco. (I, 2)
>
> Dilatada llanura rodeada de altas montañas: a lo lejos se descubre otra parte del lago. (I, 8)
>
> Esterior de una gruta. (II, 1)
>
> Cámara del palacio de Sterlinga. (II, 9)

Il Contestabile di Chester:

> Interior del castillo de la Montaña: baluartes que circuyen la fortaleza: torres que les dominan: puerta cerrada. (I, 1)
>
> Oyese el sonido de clarines militares: se levanta lienzo de la tienda, y se descubre la llanura que domina el castillo de la montaña, cubierta de pueblo y de los ejércitos de Sacy, y de los caballeros Cruzados... (I, 6)
>
> Gran peñasco, con un torrente profundo, por el cual pasa un puente. Una abertura natural conduce a lugares subterráneos. (II, 4)

A la derecha del actor se ve una antigua capilla arruinada. En lo violento de una tempestad aparece el Condestable embozado en una capa de hermitaño . . . (III, 1)

The Italian opera turned to the literature and history of all ages and all countries for sources for its librettos, and naturally turned to Scott. Only two of the Scott-derived operas, however, *Lucia di Lamermoor* and *I Puritani,* achieved any lasting place in the repertory; but *La Donna del lago* and *Il Contestabile di Chester* were two of the many operas in the pre-Romantic years that pointed the way to more elaborate staging and scenic effects which were to reach a new level of excellence and detailed realism in the drama with the presentation of Martínez de la Rosa's *Conjuración de Venecia.*

The University of North Carolina

---

[1] For studies on Scott's vogue and influence in Spain see: Philip H. Churchman and E. Allison Peers, "A Survey of the Influence of Sir Walter Scott in Spain," *Revue Hispanique,* LXV (1922), 227-310; and E. Allison Peers, "Studies in the Influence of Sir Walter Scott in Spain," *Revue Hispanique,* LXVIII (1926), 1-160.

[2] Churchman and Peers, *op. cit.,* 268-69.

[3] *Sir Walter Scott's Novels on the Stage,* (New Haven, 1927).

[4] Emilio Cotarelo y Mori, *Orígenes y establecimiento de la ópera en España hasta 1800* (Madrid, 1917).

[5] Luis Carmena y Millán, *Crónica de la ópera italiana en Madrid desde el año 1738 hasta nuestros días* (Madrid, 1878), P. 51.

[6] The influence of the Italian opera on Spanish Romanticism will be presented in a longer study.

[7] Bilingual text, Italian and Spanish, Madrid: Sancha, 1837.

[8] Bilingual text, Italian and Spanish, Madrid: Sancha, 1831.

[9] Bilingual text, Italian and Spanish, Madrid: Tomás Jordán, 1835.

[10] Bilingual text, Italian and Spanish, Madrid: Sancha, 1836.

[11] Bilingual text, Italian and Spanish, Madrid: Sancha, 1837.

[12] Bilingual text, Italian and Spanish, Madrid: Imp. Teatro de la Cruz, 1841; Madrid: Boix, 1845.

The Critics and *O Missionario*

THE CRITICS AND *O MISSIONARIO*
Don H. Walther

In the study of Latin American literature, the years between the two great world conflicts were years in which scholars, in the main, became acquainted with and evaluated the more evident works—those works which won general recognition soon after publication. For example, a glance at the titles of theses written in the United States on Latin American literature indicates how much emphasis has been placed on relatively few authors and works. Many duplications have been the result.[1] Even the writers of the histories of Latin American literature have usually been content to devote their discussion to the best known authors and works. If they have sought to go further, the results have amounted to little more than lists of names.

Certainly the time has come for a revaluation of the works of better known authors, and for critical appraisal of works by lesser known authors who, for reasons not always explainable, have remained unknown or been unjustly forgotten. It might be found, for example, that consideration of *Mis enlutadas* of Gutiérrez Nájera would have much more significance than the ever recurring references to the *Sonata de Schubert* or the *De blanco;* or, again, as Torres Rioseco has suggested, that the greatest poems of Darío are those subsequent to his *Cantos de vida y esperanza.*[2] Of those works with great intrinsic merit which have never gained their rightful position, the Brazilian novel *O Missionário* by Herculano Marcos Inglêz de Souza is an example well worth attention.[3] How it is that so excellent a novel remained an obscure book for nearly half a century is not easily understood.

Inglêz de Souza was not an unknown figure in the politial and intellectual life of Brazil. He occupied the chair of Juridical and Social Sciences in the *Faculdade de Direito* in Rio de Janeiro. Later on he was appointed *presidente* of Sergipe. From there he moved to the same high position in the government of Espíritu Santo. Thereafter he continued to serve his country as deputy to the federal legislature. He was also closely connected with the leading literary figures of his time. In 1895 the publication of the *Revista Brasileira* was resumed. In its editorial offices Machado de Assis, José Veríssimo, Graça Aranha, Inglêz de Souza, and others, met frequently, and the Brazilian Academy of Letters was organized by this group in 1897. Inglêz de Souza was one of the charter members.[4]

As a novelist, Inglêz de Souza has not enjoyed the success which he encountered in other endeavors. That the first edition of *O Missionário* could have been overlooked is understandable. It was written in 1888 and published in Santos in 1891 under the pseudonym of Luiz Dolzani.[5] The second edition appeared in Rio in 1899. Why it should have fared so badly is not easily seen. For some insight into the matter, one naturally looks for the comments of the three most influential critics of Brazilian literature at the turn of the century: Sylvio Romero, Araripe Junior, and José Veríssimo.

Two editions of Sylvio Romero's *História da Literatura Brasileira* were published during Romero's life. The first appeared in 1888, too early to consider *O Missionário*. The second edition was published in 1902, but it, too, has no reference to the novel. This is also true of the third edition (published posthumously), which included additional studies by the author.

The second critic mentioned above, Araripe Junior, was at least acquainted with the novel. He wrote a prologue for the 1899 edition of the work. This prologue considers many aspects of the book; but most important, from an historical point of view, it places Inglêz de Souza among the Brazilian novelists whom the author judges to be the most talented: Aluizio Azevedo, Raul Pompéia, and Coelho Neto. Araripe Junior expresses himself in a definite manner: "O Dr. Inglês de Souza ... tem incontestavelmente direito a sentar-se entre os mestres do que surgem ..."[6]

Since Araripe Junior's comments were published as a prologue to the novel, they could have reached no wider audience than did the novel itself. That is not true, however, of the appraisal of José Veríssimo. Probably no critic of Brazilian literature has had more influence or reached a greater number of readers than he. His basic studies on Brazilian literature were published in six volumes between 1901 and 1910. These studies were followed in 1916 by his *História da Literatura Brasileira*. Veríssimo's attitude towards *O Missionário*, however, is difficult to explain; but this, nonetheless, may account to some degree for the books' reaching so few.

In the volume of the *Estudos* published in 1903, Veríssimo devotes to *O Missionário* a chapter written subsequently to the second edition of the novel. He states that the first edition of the work had appeared in a form not suited to its class of literature, that it had reached very few, and that it had remained undeservedly wthout recognition. In a more positive manner, Veríssimo writes as follows: "... não hesito em affirmar, [the novel is] um dos melhores,, ao meu parecer, da nossa ficção em prosa ... a impressão geral ... é o [sic] de uma obra quasi perfeita ..."[7] "Não creio que a naturalismo tenha produzido no Brazil obra superior a esta ..."[8] He closes his remarks by pointing out some of the faults of the novel as he sees them, and by praising Inglêz de Souza for not adopting the many abuses of the naturalistic school which, he says, are apparent in Aluízio Azevedo's *O Homem* and Julio Ribeiro's novel *A Carne*.

With the above comments in mind, it is surprising to find that Veríssimo seems to have completely forgotten *O Missionário* in his *História da Literatura Brasileira*. Indeed, there is no mention whatsoever of Inglêz de Souza in the history. Of Brazilian prose fiction in the naturalistic vein, Veríssimo has this to say: "Obras realmente notaveis e vivedouras, ou sequer estimaveis, bem poucas produziu, e nomes que mereçam historiados são, acaso, apenas tres: Aluizio de Azevedo, Julio Ribeiro e Raul Pompeia."[9]

What caused the change in Veríssimo's attitude or made him forget the novel can only be conjectured. The fact is that during most of the first half of this century *O Missionário* was forgotten. One looks in vain for any reference to the work or its author in the well known history of Brazilian literature by Ronald de Carvalho. In this country, Isaac Goldberg, who depended considerably on Veríssimo and Carvalho, gives no evidence that he was acquainted with *O Missionário*. An examination of other manuals and of literary periodicals for comments on the novel or its author is likewise unprofitable.

In 1938 Olívio Montenegro re-examined the novel, judiciously placing it among the best works in Brazilian fiction. By this time, however, a copy of the novel was difficult to obtain. Nearly forty years had passed since the publication of the second edition. A new printing was needed before it could be widely known. The publishing house of José Olympio in Rio filled the need by publishing in 1946 a third edition based on the first two.

The favorable appraisal of the novel by a respected critic, and the publication of a new edition of the work now facilitates its reconsideration. In fact, a majority of the appraisals of the Brazilian novel now include a comment on *O Missionário*, although many such comments still indicate only a second hand knowledge of the work.

The University of North Carolina

[1] For a list of such duplications see L. L. Barrett, "Theses Dealing with Hispano-American Language and Literature—1948," *Hispania*, XXXII (1949), p. 148.

[2] See A. Torres Rioseco, *New World Literature* (Berkeley: Univ. of California Press, 1949), p. 148.

[3] The author's name is sometimes spelled Inglês de Sousa.

[4] See Lucia Miguel Pereira, *Machado de Assis* (3a ed., São Paulo: Cia Editora Nacional, 1946), p. 238 f.

[5] See "Introdução" by Aurélio Buarque de Hollanda in H. Inglêz de Souza, *O Missionário* (3a ed., Rio: José Olympio, 1946), p. ix.

[6] See "Prólogo" by Araripe Junior in Inglêz de Souza, *O Missionário*, p. 24.

[7] José Veríssimo, *Estudos de Literatura Brazileira* (Rio: H. Garnier, 1903), p. 22.

[8] *Ibid.*, p. 31.

[9] José Veríssimo, *História da Literatura Brasileira* (Rio: Francisco Alves, 1916), p. 354.

A Note on the Identity of Marie de France

A NOTE ON THE IDENTITY OF MARIE DE FRANCE
Rogers Dey Whichard

One of the most fascinating problems of the medieval literary historian is that of the indentification of Marie de France. Some years ago Professor U. T. Holmes, Jr., enumerated an illustrious list of scholars on both sides of the Atlantic who have investigated this problem and have published their findings or conjectures.[1] In the same article, Holmes presented an ingenious theory for the identification of Marie, which has intrigued the present writer for some time because of its simple logic and plausibility. Recent research has brought to light additional information having a bearing on Holmes's theory, and it is proposed to review here the basis of his identification and to present data which may in some way corroborate it.

We start with what are the three most universally accepted facts concerning Marie's life: that she was born in the Ile-de-France or one of its dependencies, that she was of noble birth, and that she lived and composed her works in England. One individual was found who fits in with all these qualifications, and she is Marie, the eighth child of Waleran de Meulan (I use the Norman form of his given name for reasons which will later be obvious) and of Agnès de Montfort. This Marie was born at Saint-Germain-en-Laye close to the middle of the twelfth century, and married Hugh Talbot, baron de Cleuville.[2] It is shown further that Talbot owned land in Hereford and north Devon, two localities rich in Celtic lore and tradition, the former being adjacent to Monmouth and South Wales and the latter the supposed location of King Arthur's castle, Camelot. So it appears that Marie, daughter of Waleran, was a native of the Ile-de-France, was of noble birth, and probably resided at least part of the time in England on her husband's estates or at court. Further, she had access to and was probably familiar with the Celtic legends of which Marie de France wrote so beautifully. Here the identification by Holmes stops.

But we can go further. The countship of Meulan was only one of the fiefs of Waleran. His more usual appellation was Waleran de Beaumont (to which estate he succeeded at the death of his father), and he was member of a well-known family holding lands on both sides of the English Channel. His grandfather, Roger de Beaumont (fl. early eleventh century), married the daughter of an older Waleran, count of Meulan. Robert de Beaumont, son of Roger, inherited the countship of Meulan upon failure of the direct male line, fought at Hastings, became lord of Leicester, and died in 1118. He had three sons: Waleran, Robert, and Hugh, who became respectively count of Meulan (this was Marie's father), earl of Leicester, and earl of Bedford. It is of passing interest that Waleran and Robert were twins and were born in 1104. It is also of passing interest that the earldom of Leicester passed into the Montfort family (but at a later date) by the marriage of Robert's daughter to Simon (III) de Montfort, her brother having died without issue. Of more importance to us is the fact that Waleran de Beaumont, count of Meulan, was also earl of Worcester.[3] Thus Marie de Beaumont (as I shall now call her) had much stronger ties with England than formerly appeared. Not only did her husband own estates in that country, but so did her father and two uncles: in Worcester, Leicester, and Bedford. The two latter localities are not significant here, but her father's earldom of Worcester is particularly so, since it adjoins Hereford not far from the Welsh border.

It has been pointed out that topographical references in the *Lais* of Marie de France are very limited, if we except those in *Eliduc*, *Milon*, and *Yonec* (Totnes, Exeter, Caerlon, Caerwent, and South Wales). However, there are others which will, I believe, take on special significance in view of what we have seen above. In *Les deus amanz* there is reference to the town and valley of Pitres (Pistres) in such definite terms that it would seem almost certain the poet was acquainted with it. Hoepffner tell us[4] that the legend of the two lovers is strictly localized near Pont-de-l'Arche. Glancing at a map, we may see for ourselves the town of Pitres just to the north of Pont-de-l'Arche near the confluence of the Seine and the Andelle.[5] Let us see how Marie de France refers to this locality:

> ... Une cité fist fere uns rois
> Qui estoit sire des Pistrois.
> Des Pistrois la fist [il] nomer,
> Et Pistre la fist apeler.
> Toz jors a puis duré li nons;
> Encor i a vile et mesons.
> Nos savon bien de la contrée
> Que le val de Pitre est nommée.
>   (*Les Deus Amanz*, lines 13-20.)
> Devers Seine, en la praerie ...
>   (*Ibid.*, line 180.)

What could be more specific? To know that the name still endured in her day, that there were still houses and a town, that there was a meadow down toward the Seine, the poet must have been familiar with the locality. The significance of this is that less than fifty kilometers to the southwest is Beaumont-le-Roger, and a little farther to the east are Meulan, Saint-Germain-en-Laye, and Montfort-l'Amaury, within a radius of fifteen kilometers of each other. These are all places closely connected with the childhood of Marie de Beaumont: her father's ancestral home, some of his fiefs, her own birthplace, her mother's home. She could very well have been as familiar with this country and its folklore as was the author of *Les deus amanz*—she could have composed *Les deus amanz*.

One other topographical reference should be mentioned, and that occurs in *Milon*:

> A Suhthamptone vait passer.
> Comme il ainz pot, se mist en mer.
> A Barbefluet est arivez;
> Droit en Bretaigne est alez.
> (lines 317-20.)

From this we see that Marie de France knew that the safest way from South Wales (where Milon lived) to Brittany was overland to Southampton, thence by sea to Barfleur on the Cotentin peninsula, and thence again overland. It is by no means beyond the limits of probability that Marie de Beaumont had passed by the same way in traveling to and from England with her husband or other kin. Barfleur was apparently an important port in her time One authority[6] even states that the Conqueror set sail from the port for his amphibious landing at Pevensey just before the battle of Hastings in 1066, but most historians do not agree with that claim.

Since the *Lais* of Marie de France were dedicated to a king who is generally thought to have been Henry II of England, the relations of the Beaumonts with the royal house ought to throw some light on our problem. Waleran formed part of a revolt against Henry I (grandfather of Henry II) in 1123; he was captured in 1124 and was forced to surrender Beaumont, having already lost his other fiefs of Brionne and Pont-Audemer. In spite of these reverses he was present with his brother, Robert, at the deathbed of Henry on 1 December 1135. The two brothers were Stephen's chief advisers during the early years of his reign. However, Waleran made a pilgrimage to Jerusalem in 1145, and upon his return he sided with Mathilda and Henry II; in fact, he held Worcester against Stephen in 1150, at which time he was called one of Henry's chief partisans. He was at court in 1157 and was a witness to the treaty with Louis VII in 1160. Waleran died in 1166, at which time his daughter was at most sixteen years of age.[7] The literary activities of the court of Henry II are well known, and we now see that Marie de Beaumont had a connexion with that court such as Marie de France must certainly have had, if she dedicated her *Lais* to Henry II.

Marie de Beaumont was, on the distaff side, a direct descendent of Charlemagne and the Capets. Her grandmother (the wife of Robert de Beaumont who died in 1118) was Isabel of Vermandois, daughter of Hugh (brother of Philip I of the House of Capet) who was count of Vermandois in right of his wife, the heiress of Herbert IV, last of the direct male line. The previous counts in the direct succession were Herbert I (d. 902), Herbert II (d. 943), Albert I, Herbert III, Albert I, and Otto, the latter being the father of Herbert IV.[8] One authority states that Herbert II was grandson of Bernard, king of Italy, but fails to specify whether through his father or his mother.[9] Bernard (d. 818) was son of Pépin, king of Italy (d. 810), who was one of the sons of Charlemagne.[10]

We also know something of the heraldry of the Beaumonts. There is in existence a seal of Waleran of about 1136-38, showing shield, trapper and flag chequy. This apparently derives from Vermandois, since his mother's brother, Ralph, count of Vermandois, used the same design on two seals of 1135 and 1146. It is interesting that the earls of Surrey, whose ancestor, William de Warenne, married Isabel of Vermandois after the death of Robert de Beaumont, used the chequy shield also. Of course, the tinctures of the shields do not show on a seal, so it is not until the blazon of John de Warenne, earl of Surrey, is shown on a roll of 1298, that we know the coat to be "chequy or and azure." The chequy coat of Vermandois is said to be one of the oldest known to heraldry.[11]

We are still far from proving the identity of Marie de France with Marie de Beaumont. All we can say now is that the respective facts concerning them are not contradictory. If, some fortunate person is able to forge the link which will prove their identity, then Marie de France has waiting for her an illustrious background worthy of her great literary talent and accomplishments.

Norfolk Division,
College of William and Mary—V. P. I.

[1] *Studies in Philology*, XXIX (1932), 1-10.
[2] *Op cit.*, pp. 6-7.
[3] DNB, II, 64-70 *et passim*.
[4] E. Hoepfner, ed. *Les lais de Marie de France* (Strasbourg: Heitz, 1921), p.x. Quotations which we give from the *Lais* are from this edition.
[5] *Larousse universel* under *Pitres* and *Eure*. See also U. T. Holmes, Jr. in *Symposium*, III (1949), 335-39.
[6] *Larousse universel*, under *Barfleur*.
[7] DNB, II, 69-70; Enc. Brit. (11th ed.), XVIII, 1042.
[8] Enc. Brit., XXVII, 1024; DNB, II, 66.
[9] *Cambridge Medieval History*, III, 76.
[10] James Westfall Thompson, *The Middle Ages, 300-1500* (New York: Knopf, 1932), pp. 278, 283.
[11] Anthony R. Wagner, F. S. A., *Historic Heraldry of Britain* (London; New York; Toronto: Oxford University Press, 1948), p. 46.

A Defense of the Renaissance
Gentilhomme Champetre

A DEFENSE OF THE RENAISSANCE *GENTILHOMME CHAMPETRE*

W. L. Wiley

From the reign of Francis I until the end of the sixteenth century in France, court life became progressively lavish and a *gentilhomme* wanted to be near his king. This is certainly one theme of the poets from Marot to Ronsard, though occasional pastoral notes are added for contrast. The same theme is present in the *mémoires* and commentaries of chroniclers like Fleurange, Martin and Guillaume du Bellay, Pierre de l'Estoile, Brantôme, Montluc and others. The court is the place where a nobleman wins distinction and finds satisfaction. The son of a nobleman should gain experience and knowledge, even as did Bayard, at some minor court (possibly first as a page), and thus prepare himself for later entrance into the king's own atmosphere. The ultimate goal was to render military and social service to the monarch. It could mean, of course, that the *gentilhomme* might have to abandon his own estates in the provinces, but it was worth such an upheaval to bask in the effulgence of the king. This was the general opinion as expressed by the poets and historians, and the *déracinement* of the nobility became more and more evident as the century progressed.[1] The *cahier* of the *tiers état* of the *Etats-Généraux* of 1576 complains, for example, that the king's retinue is now so filled with nobles that it is a great burden to whatever province of the land the king may choose to favor with his presence. The burden is all the greater because every "petit courtisan, jusques à un simple archer de la garde" has his wife with him, trailing after the king.[2] A separate *noblesse de cour* is in the process of development.

Some dissenting voices were heard in the second half of the century, though more and more *gentilshommes* are coming to Paris and the king's court. The *conteurs* take a more rural and earthly point of view, and Noël du Fail, in his *Contes et discours d'Eutrapel*, published in 1585, speaks of courts and their unhealthy effects upon the country *gentilhomme*, who has been accustomed on his lands to a simpler and healthier life.[3] Earlier, Charles Estienne in his detailed work on a *gentilhomme*'s house and estates, *L'agriculture et maison rustique*,[4] praises the soil and agriculture. He says that Roman consuls and senators loved "la culture de la terre" and that the same is true of "plusieurs grands seigneurs de notre temps." It should be mentioned, says Estienne, that "feu Roy François, père des sciences" encouraged "peregrinations" to enrich France with "plusieurs plantes, herbes, et arbres exquis" that were unknown before.[5] Then complete directions are given for the construction of the manor house, servants' quarters, stables, gardens, orchards, pastures, etc. Estienne urges that the master of this establishment live in it rather than " à la ville," and that he spend his time " à philosopher et entendre au gouvernement du sien" rather than in hunting and drunken parties.[6] This same note concerning the responsibilities of the country gentleman is repeated by Olivier de Serres in his *Théâtre d'agriculture et mesnage des champs*, first published in 1600. Both he and Estienne call the owner of an estate "le père de famille" and insist that his attitude toward all those around him should be paternal. Serres' book, which borrows a great deal from Estienne's work, had several editions in the seventeenth century.

A most delightful poetic defense of the country gentleman—and the *raison d'être* of this little article—is to be found in *Les plaisirs du gentilhomme champestre*, attributed to Nicolas Rapin and published in 1583.[7] The poem is made up of sixty-five 5-line stanzas, an unusual poetic form for the period, in praise of the life of the *gentilhomme champêtre*. The general suggestion is toward a moderately epicurean enjoyment of life, and that enjoyment, like that of Horace in his *Beatus ille* . . . , is not to be looked for in the noisy crowds. The pleasures of the *gentilhomme champêtre* come from, among other things, his hunting, his crops, his wine, his dogs, moderate food, and from his absence from the pomp and grandeur of the court.

It is a fine thing for the *gentilhomme* in the country to be far from the marts of trade, to cultivate his own fields where there is never any question concerning his position:

> Heureux celuy qui loing d'affaires
> Comme les gens du temps passé
> Avec ses boeufs ordinaires
> Laboure les champs, que ses peres
> En propre luy ont delaissé.
>
> De qui la noblesse cognue
> Ne vient iamais en question
> Mais de longue main est tenue,
> Comme si elle estoit venue
> D'un des enfants de Francion.[8]

His house should be comfortable but not too sumptuous, with meadows, woodlands, and a pond, even as Estienne had suggested:

> De qui la maison est bastie
> > Sans grande sumptuosité:
> > De peu de logis assortie:
> > Belle entree et belle sortie
> > Avec toute commodité.
>
> De qui la terre bien bornee
> > Se ioint au clos de la maison:
> > De prez et garenne entouree
> > D'un bois & d'un estang ornee
> > Et d'une faye en la cloison.[8]

With his restricted preserve (the *garenne* above) and his beech-tree in his enclosure, the *gentilhomme champêtre* is a happy man:

> Qui n'a point en son voisinage
> > Un prince ny grand Seigneur:
> > Mais seul commande en son vilage
> > Sans s'obliger à d'avantage,
> > Qu'à vivre selon son humeur.[8]

The independence of the provincial noble of the earlier part of the century is reflected in the above lines. And, along with other privileges of his position, he might take a walk through the fields and meet a *bergère*:

> Et si par fortune il rencontre
> > La bergere un peu à l'escart,
> > Le doux ieu d'amour il luy monstre,
> > Où (*sic*) se contente de la monstre
> > S'il n'y peut avoir plus grand part.[9]

However, in addition to these amusements *en passant*, it is very nice if he has "une femme non importune" waiting for him at home at the end of the day, like "celles du viel age,"[10] with supper ready and a smile on her face:

> Heureux si venant de la chasse
> > Ou d'ailleurs, il trouve tout prest,
> > Son souper cuit de bonne grace,
> > Avec une riante face
> > Qui plus que les vivres luy plaist.[11]

Happy is he also who has his horses in his stables, a variety of dogs and the more gentle hunting birds around him. Note that specific numbers are given—*trois chevaux, six chiens courants*, and *deux levriers*:

> Qui a trois chevaux en l'estable
> > Six chiens courants et deux levriers,
> > Six espagneux: et pour la table,

> L'autour ou le lanier traictable,
> Sans faulcons & sans esperviers.[12]

The *gentilhomme champêtre*, if we may believe the *conteurs* and the chroniclers, was not a man of highly developed literary tastes.[13] However, sometimes on a winter's evening, well wrapped up in warm clothes, he might become interested in a good book:

> Quelquefois de tout soin delivre
> D'un plus chault habit revestu,
> Il list dedans quelque bon livre
> Qui monstre comment il faut suivre
> Le beau chemin de la vertu.[14]

There will be found on his table partridges and capons and "des pigeons du colombier"—not exactly a frugal meal by modern standards—but there will be no display of peacocks and pheasants in the lavish manner of the court. The *gentilhomme's* repasts will be modest affairs with his friends, without any aftermath of hiccoughs, apothecary's drugs, or doctor's visits:

> Leur repas est libre et modeste
> D'herbes & de fruicts meslangé:
> N'engendrent un hocquet moleste,
> Qui volontiers aux banquets reste
> Apres que l'on a trop mangé.
>
> Aussi ne leur faut-il point faire
> Tant de despens en Medecin,
> Ny en drogues d'apotiquaire:
> Ainsi personne à leur affaire
> Ne vient espier le bassin.
>
> Qui est celuy qui eust envie
> Manger des Paons & des phaisans,
> Et changer ceste heureuse vie
> A la friandise asservie
> Des miserables courtisans?[15]

In the country the *gentilhomme* will be free from a lot of the sartorial problems of the court, like changing clothes every day and bothering to make his breath smell sweet:

> Aussi n'avez-vous point la peine
> De vous friser tout le matin:
> De faire bien sentir l'haleine,
> Et chaque jour de la sepmaine
> Changer de veloux & satin.

> De gaudronner vostre chemise
> Et toujours y porter la main:
> De vous habiller à la guise
> Tantost d'un Seigneur de Venise
> Tantost d'un chevalier Romain.[16]

The poem goes on to the conclusion that a *gentilhomme*, by avoiding the excesses of the court and carrying on this well-modulated fashion of living "aux champs," could reach the ripe old age of one hundred years.

The *Plaisirs du gentilhomme champestre* is certainly not a great piece of literature. It is far from being a significant or important poem, though it does have an easy and relaxed quality. By its publication, it in no sense of the word hastened a departure from the court back to the soil. This would have been too great an expectation, as Vaissière has put it, from "le pouvoir de la poésie."[17] However, the *Plaisirs du gentilhomme champestre* does suggest most entertainingly that a *gentilhomme*, a long way from Henri III and his *mignons*, could have a good time living in the country.

The University of North Carolina

---

[1] Pierre de Vaissière in his *Gentilshommes campagnards de l'ancienne France* (Paris: Perrin, 1903), p. 180 ff., puts the real uprooting of the *gentilhomme* from his lands at around 1575.

[2] Chérin, *La noblesse considérée sous ses divers rapports, dans les assemblées générales et particulières de la nation* .... (Paris, 1788), p. 153.

[3] Noël du Fail, *Contes et discours d'Eutrapel* (Paris: Bibliothéque Elzévirienne, 1874), I, 245 ff; II, 162 ff. In the second excerpt a strong *défense* is made for the simpler manners of former times.

[4] Charles Estienne, *L'agriculture et maison rustique* (Paris: J. Du Puis, 1564); 155 folios, plus Table.

[5] All these short quotations are from the *epistre* at the beginning of Estienne's work. It was written to the *conseiller du Roy*, and is dated 15 jan. 1564.

[6] Estienne, *op. cit.*, chap. 5.

[7] Nicolas Rapin, *Les plaisirs du gentil homme champestre* (Paris: Veuve Lucas Breyer, 1583); 33 folios. The poem has no author's name except the initials, N. R. P. At the end of the book are some verses from Seigneur de Pybrac, Cl. Binet, and Ronsard.

[8] *Les plaisirs du gentilhomme champestre*, pp. 5 verso-6 recto.

[9] *Ibid.*, p. 8 recto.

[10] *Ibid.*, p. 9 verso.

[11] *Ibid.*, p. 10 recto.

[12] *Ibid.*, p. 6 recto.

[13] Something of the literary tastes of the *gentilhomme* on his estates is indicated in Noël du Fail (*op. cit.*, II, 169), where a small quantity of books

is cited. The matter of a *gentilhomme*'s reading is taken up also by La Noue, *Discours politiques et militaires* (Basle: François Forest, 1587), in the fifth and sixth *discours*.

[14] *Les plaisirs du gentilhomme champestre*, p. 10 verso.

[15] *Ibid.*, pp. 11 verso-12 recto. Does "espier le bassin" in the middle stanza suggest the possibility of poisoned wine?

[16] *Ibid.*, pp. 12 verso-13 recto.

[17] Vaissière, *op. cit.*, p. 214.

Sarrazins Espans in the *Roland*, vv. 269, 612, 2828

SARRAZINS ESPANS IN THE *ROLAND*, VV. 269, 612, 2828

William S. Woods

Editors and scholars of *la Chanson de Roland* have been in almost universal agreement that the adjective *espans*, lines 269, 612, and 2828, used as a qualifier of the Saracens should be interpreted as "Spanish." Boissonnade, who seems to have discussed the word at greater length than anyone else, says[1]:

> Ce sont eux (les Almoravides) que le poète distingue nettement des musulmans d'Espagne, mélange d'Arabes, de Syriens, de Maghrebins, d'indigènes, et qu'il nomme les *Sarrazins Espans* (Espagnols), tandis que les annalistes latins les distinguent sous le nom de *Sarraceni*, de *Mauri*, d'*Argeni*.

While it is true in a general sense that *espans* in the three lines in question signified "Spanish," the term had a more restricted meaning for a number of years before, and possibly after, the time of the *Roland*. Examination of some of the early documents of Spain will reveal that the adjective referred to *Musulman Spain* only.

Menéndez Pidal, quoting the *Crónica Albeldense*, helps to fix the exact significance of the word in his statement[2]:

> Ordoño I se preocupó de las inmediatas (ciudades abandonadas), amurallando y restaurando a León (856), Astorga, Túy y Amaya (860), ciudades que pobló de cristianos del Norte y de Mozárabes, o, como dice el cronista (Albeldense), las llenó de gentes venidas en parte de su reino y en parte de "España" ("partem ex suis, partim *ex Spania* advenientibus"): sabido es que cuando casi la totalidad cayó bajo la dominación extranjera, la voz *Hispania* fué, para los cristianos independientes, sinónima de tierra musulmana.

In the passage quoted from the Albeldense chronicle, the author is obviously making a clear distinction between Ordoño's land and *Spania*.

Lévi-Provençal makes a similar statement, although he does not inform us as to the sources of his information[3]:

> Pour les non-musulmans, le Sud de l'Espagne portait au moyen-âge le nom d'Hispania ou de Spania, tandis que les principautés chrétiennes proche de la barrière pyrénéenne, la Galice, les Asturies, la Castille, Léon, la Navarre, la Catalogne, n'avient point d'appellation commune et étaient désignées sous leurs noms particuliers.

In his *La España del Cid*, Menéndez Pidal gives several quotations from other early Spanish documents which help to prove that the term *Hispania* referred to the Moorish section of Spain alone at the time of the *Chanson de Roland*[4]:

> P. 886, note 2: En 1083 el Conde Urgel pensaba en adquisiciones en Almenar, "de la serra d'Almenara versus Ispaniam" (Ispania—tierra de Moros) Villanueva, *Viaje literar.* XII (1850), p. 232.
>
> P. 946, from the *Historia Roderici*: Comes (Berenguer) autem Yspanie partem quandam suo imperio subditam in protectione et in manu Roderici tunc posuit; pariter itaque ambo ad loca maritima sibi proxima ilico descenderunt.

Volume VI of the *Cambridge Medieval History* refers to this transaction as follows (p. 401): "Moreover Rodrigo was granted the protectorate over the Muslim provinces south-west of Catalonia, in place of the Catalan count who had been so unfortunate in war." Menéndez Pidal identifies still more precisely those parts of "Spanie" which were placed under Rodrigo's protection.

> Pp. 415-416: . . . el conde renunciaba formalmente a las tierras del difunto Alhaŷib, que de antiguo le pagaban tributo, las que con tanto esfuerzo había querido estorbar al Campeador, y las colocaba ahora bajo la protección de éste . . . Al morir Alhaŷib había dejado un hijo pequeño, Çuleiman Ben Hud, bajo la tutela de los Ben Betir: uno de éstos tenía a Denia, donde residía el muchacho y donde acuñaba su moneda; otro tenía a Játiva, otro a Tortosa, y los tres convinieron en que, abandonados por Berenguer, no podían pasar sin la amistad del Cid, por lo que le enviaron a decir con el mayor rendimiento que haría cuanto él tuviese por bien. El Campeador les fijó 50 000 dinares cada año, y ellos aceptaron, poniendo bajo su protección toda la tierra de Lérida y Tortosa, así como la de Denia hasta Orihuela.
>
> P. 954, from the *Historia Roderici*: Nisi vero cito venisset, ille barbare gentes Yspani (am) totam usque ad Caesaraugustam et Leridam jam preoccupassent, atque omnino obtinuissent.
>
> P. 955, from the *Historia Roderici*: Sermo quidem iste omnibus Valentiae hominibus placuit. Ad Iuzeph et ad omnes Yspaniarum duces quicumque erant sub imperio Iuzeph, litteras suas continuo miserunt, in quibus, ut cum inmenso exercitu ad Valentiam venirent et de manu Roderici et de eius imperio eosdem liberarent, eis notificaverunt.
>
> P. 891, from the Latin *Carmen* on the Cid, ll. 65-68:
> Iubet e terra virum exulare;
> hinc cepit ipse Mauros debellare,
> Ispaniarum patrias vastare,
> urbes delere.
>
> P. 753, from a notarial formula: En los documentos privados de Sahagún hallamos una fórmula empleada, durante muchos años, por los notarios y usada rutinariamente sin comprenderla: "regnante rex domno Adefonso in Toleto et imperante Christianorum quam et paganorum omnia Hispanie regna," 25 enero 1098.

These passages seem to indicate that from the ninth to the early twelfth century the term *Hispania* referred to the provinces of Spain dominated by the Arabs, as opposed to the northern Christian Provinces.

It is even possible to fix the dates of this limited meaning of the word *espans* a little more definitely. Menéndez Pidal contents himself with a rather general statement about the dates of the restriction of meaning. On p. 72 he says:

> El nombre mismo de *Spania* está entonces a punto de desnaturalizarse, pues tiende a designar especialmente el país islamizado, por ser éste la mayor parte de la Península, mientras los pequeños Estados cristianos operan en el Norte aislados, por lo común, unos de otros.

His reference is to the early years of the Arab invasion of Spain. Whether or not this is true at such an early date we cannot say. However we can be sure that by the middle of the ninth century *Hispania* designated the lands under Arab domination. It was during that century that the Crónica Albeldense was written and this is the first use of the term in that sense that I have encountered. This would supply a definite *terminus a quo*, though it is possible that the restriction in meaning began earlier. The *terminus ad quem* is more difficult to arrive at, but there are some indications which suggest a date for the end of the restricted meaning of *espans*. Menéndez Pidal notes (p. 751) that in the year 1077 is the beginning of the use of the genitive *totius Spanie* in the title of the king. "Ego Adefonsus totius Ispanie rex" is first noted in 1077 and it is found again in 1079. In 1081 he finds the following title, "Ego Adefonsus sub gratia Dei Hispaniarum princeps." By this date, then, the term is again referring to Spain as a whole, although some years were to pass before the restricted sense of the word died out completely. The *Historia Roderici* uses the word with the limited meaning and it dates probably from the early years of the twelfth century.

The author of the *Chanson de Roland* is obviously using *espans* in its limited meaning, for in all three cases where it occurs in the poem it is employed as what Bédier calls an "épithète de Sarrasin." Further, the dating of the restricted sense coincides perfectly with the dates commonly ascribed to the oldest extant version of the *Roland*.[5] The *Sarrazins espans* in the three lines of the *Roland* were, then, Saracens from Mozarabic Spain.[6]

Tulane University

[1] P. Boissonnade, *Du nouveau sur la Chanson de Roland* (Paris: Champion, 1923), p. 154.

[2] R. Menéndenz Pidal, *El idioma español en sus primeros tiempos* (Buenos Aires: Espasa-Calpe, 1945), p. 52.

[3] E. Lévi-Provençal, *L'Espagne musulmane au Xe siècle* (Paris: Larose, 1932), p. 6.

[4] R. Menéndez Pidal, *La España del Cid* (Madrid: Editorial Plutarco, 1929).

[5] Godefroy cites one additional appearance of this word, in the *Chanson d'Antioche* (VIII, 1011, P. Paris): "Corbaran i couchierent en un lit d'or espan." Paris translates it as "brilliant," but Godefroy defines it as "d'Espagne."

[6] Bédier, whose version of the poem I have followed, changes the *en Espaigne* of line 269 to *espan* for reasons of assonance.

SUBSCRIBERS
To April 15, 1950

Nicholson B. Adams
Raymond Andes
H. L. Ballew
J. Worth Banner
L. L. Barrett
William H. Baskin III
R. S. Boggs
Wallace R. Brandon
Charles B. Brockmann
John E. Carroll, Jr.
Walter D. Creech
Sue Johnson Dale
John A. Downs
Edward T. Draper-Savage
Frank W. Duffey
Alfred Engstrom
Bettie Sue Gardner
Rosalyn Gardner
Hugo Giduz
Marion A. Greene
Jacques Hardré
Mrs. Willis Banks Harris
Elliott D. Healy
Urban T. Holmes, Jr.
William A. Hover
Howard R. Huse
Joseph C. Hutchinson

Cecil Johnson
Lucia Porcher Johnson
Mrs. John Lipscomb Johnson
John E. Keller
George Keys
Sturgis E. Leavitt
Robert G. Lewis
J. C. Lyons
R. R. MacCurdy
William A. McKnight
John A. Moore
Edward F. Moyer
James S. Patty
W. W. Ritter, Jr.
Stanley L. Robe
Phifer P. Rothman
Jacqueline Johnson Simpson
James M. Smith
S. A. Stoudemire
William E. Strickland
Betty Sue Tilley
Bernice H. Waddell
Don H. Walther
Rogers Dey Whichard
W. L. Wiley
William S. Woods

The editors wish to express their gratitude to three friends of the Dey family who have given generous donations in order to make possible the publication of this volume. Our special thanks are due to Jane Toy Coolidge, Mrs. Crawford Johnson, Sr., and William C. Coker.

The Department of Romance Studies Digital Arts and Collaboration Lab at the University of North Carolina at Chapel Hill is proud to support the digitization of the North Carolina Studies in the Romance Languages and Literatures series.

www.ingramcontent.com/pod-product-compliance
Lightning Source LLC
Chambersburg PA
CBHW030236240426
43663CB00037B/1165